托福口语
满分攻略

Tips for Acing the
TOEFL Speaking

澜大教育集团托福教研组　编

中国科学技术大学出版社

内 容 简 介

本书为托福口语考试备考用书。托福口语作为托福考试听、说、读、写中的一项,一直是中国考生学习的难点。本书结合近5年托福口语考试真题,梳理出相关话题,帮助考生快速掌握考试必备的话题素材和回答逻辑。考生不仅可以背诵本书的话题素材丰富自己的语料库,也可以反复朗读范例答案,提升整体语感。

本书可供正在备考托福口语考试的学生使用,也可供相关教师参考阅读。

图书在版编目(CIP)数据

托福口语满分攻略/澜大教育集团托福教研组编. —合肥:中国科学技术大学出版社,2023.9
ISBN 978-7-312-05753-3

Ⅰ.托… Ⅱ.澜… Ⅲ. TOEFL—口语—自学参考资料 Ⅳ. H319.9

中国国家版本馆 CIP 数据核字(2023)第 150692 号

托福口语满分攻略
TUOFU KOUYU MANFEN GONGLÜE

出版	中国科学技术大学出版社
	安徽省合肥市金寨路 96 号,230026
	http://press. ustc. edu. cn
	https://zgkxjsdxcbs. tmall. com
印刷	安徽省瑞隆印务有限公司
发行	中国科学技术大学出版社
开本	787 mm×1092 mm 1/16
印张	14
字数	261 千
版次	2023 年 9 月第 1 版
印次	2023 年 9 月第 1 次印刷
定价	70.00 元

教研组成员

前　　言

托福考试作为申请国外大学的一项语言考试,从听、说、读、写四个板块考查考生的英文语言基础能力。其中,口语考试虽然只有 17 分钟,但是其对考生的内容逻辑、思维速度、表达能力、发音语调等方面均进行了全面考查,对于考生来说是个挑战。

在编者十几年的教学经历中,每年都有很多考生对于托福口语考试提出类似的问题:

1. 为什么我的分数一直不增长?

2. 我的发音不好是不是很难考出好成绩?

3. 想要考高分,需要练习多久?

提出这些问题的考生往往都经过了一些训练,甚至他们已经做过非常多的练习,然而这里有一个明显的问题出现了,即大家犯了欲速则不达的错误。口语考试属于一种输出性的考试,其并没有客观正确的答案,考生希望取得一个好的分数,首先应该了解获得高分需要达到哪些要求,并且是考试方给出的要求。

托福口语考试对于考生输出内容的评分,主要从三个方面进行:信息传达度、词汇语法、话题逻辑。因此结合这三个方面,有的考生分数一直不增长,往往就是因为他们只关注自己口语某一个方面的表现,比如虽然做了很多练习,对于信息传达度来说,语言很熟练、很通顺,但是话题逻辑却很混乱。又比如,即使发音不是非常标准,但是通过对词汇语法和话题逻辑的完善,也可以在评分中填补短板,获得不错的分数。

本书主要从话题逻辑和词汇语法的角度,帮助考生备考,使其打开思路并快速积累托福口语考试中最常见的话题素材。

如果考生想要考高分，需要练习多久？这个问题其实不可能存在一个标准答案，因为每个考生的语言基础是完全不一样的。但是对于所有的考生而言，都要选择正确高效的备考和练习方式，不要做重复的工作甚至是无用功。

本书结合近5年托福口语考试真题，将考试的话题题材进行了归纳、总结、梳理，可以帮助考生根据话题积累素材并进行专项练习，让考生在12个真题独立话题中，快速熟悉考试内容，在考试中可以根据话题打开思路，回答出内容丰富、逻辑清晰、用词准确的答案。此外，本书对于高频的综合任务进行了梳理。通过集中的话题集训和综合任务的文本学习，希望可以帮助考生高效备考！

编　者

2023 年 4 月

目　　录

第二部分　综合任务 Task 2～Task 4

第一部分

独立任务话题通关

Task 1

第一章　课　程　选　择

一、核心话题真题

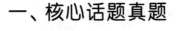

When students are reading, some choose the books from the reading list their schools give. Others choose books by themselves. Which do you prefer?

【话题解析】

课程选择类话题在托福口语独立题中出现得不算高频，但是由于大部分题目都基于美国教育背景，对中国学生来说缺少亲身经历，所以理解起来比较抽象，很难想出一些具体的例子，所以这种题目相对会难一些。这道题的意思是："当学生在阅读时，有一些人会从学校提供的书单里进行选择，而也有一些人喜欢自己挑选。你喜欢哪种方式？"我们可以总结出以下"万能"论点：

（1）更有动力阅读。

more motivated to read

（2）更放松。

more relaxed

二、核心词汇语料

passion /ˈpæʃn/   n. 热情

genre /ˈʒɑːnrə/   n. 类型

fascinate /ˈfæsɪneɪt/   v. 着迷

romance /ˈroʊmæns/   n. 爱情小说

thriller /ˈθrɪlə/   n. 惊悚小说

essay /ˈeseɪ/   n. 散文

poem /ˈpəʊɪm/   n. 诗歌

drama /ˈdrɑːmə/   n. 戏剧

physics /ˈfɪzɪks/   n. 物理

chemistry /ˈkemɪstri/   n. 化学

literature /ˈlɪtrətʃə(r)/   n. 文学

psychology /saɪˈkɑːlədʒi/   n. 心理学

biology /baɪˈɑːlədʒi/   n. 生物学

schedule /ˈskedʒuːl/   n. 日程安排

semester /sɪˈmestər/   n. 学期

department /dɪˈpɑːrtmənt/   n. 部门

leadership /ˈliːdərʃɪp/   n. 领导力

space /speɪs/   n. 空间

proposal /prəˈpəʊzl/   n. 提议

prepare /prɪˈper/   v. 准备

disruptive /dɪsˈrʌptɪv/   adj. 破坏性的

concentrate /ˈkɑːnsntreɪt/   v. 集中

assignment /əˈsaɪnmənt/   n. 任务

handout /ˈhændaʊt/ *n*. 讲义

seminar /ˈsemɪnɑːr/ *n*. 研讨会

program /ˈprəʊɡræm/ *n*. 项目

credit /ˈkredɪt/ *n*. 学分

major /ˈmeɪdʒər/ *n*. 专业；*v*. 专业

drastic /ˈdræstɪk/ *adj*. 剧烈的

a variety of 多种多样的

classic music 古典音乐

graduation requirement 毕业要求

get involved in 参与

exchange ideas 交换想法

review for final exams 为期末考试而复习

prepare for class 为上课做准备

course material 课程材料

academic building 教学楼

release pressure 释放压力

be addicted to 被……吸引

best seller 畅销书

detective story 侦探小说

三、满分回答 Sample

When students are reading, some choose the books from the reading list their schools give. Others choose books by themselves. Which do you prefer?

观点 Personally，I believe that it's better for students to choose books by themselves.

论点 1：Firstly，choosing the books myself would motivate me to read. For example，last semester I chose a famous detective book from Agatha. I was so addicted to the tense storyline in this novel that I read the entire novel in one sitting，which took me two days to finish the whole book.

论点 2：Secondly，I can be more relaxed. I mean，it's obvious that students are quite busy with their schoolwork every day，dealing with assignments and preparing for midterms and finals. So，students will cherish the opportunity to take a break and enjoy their valuable free time by choosing what they really want to read.

四、变形题思路解析

1 Should parents discourage children from choosing some majors which might be very competitive to find a job in the future?

选择 disagree：

(1) 孩子自己选择会更有动力去学习。

Children will be more motivated to learn if they choose for themselves.

(2) 有竞争力的专业往往会有较高的收入。

Competitive majors usually have higher salaries.

观点 In my opinion，parents should not interfere with the student's decisions for the following reasons.

论点 1：Firstly, students would have motivation and initiative to work if they choose the majors on their own. For example，my cousin chose to major in medicine in college，which his parents did not agree with. But he worked very hard. He spent a lot of time reading medical literature and went to many hospitals to intern. Now，he is a successful doctor.

论点 2：Secondly, competitive jobs usually have higher salaries. To be more specific, people engaged in highly competitive jobs like doctors, businessmen, sales agents could earn more money compared with other careers. So they are more likely to have a better life.

2 Should students choose their own courses，or should the professor assign the courses to them?

选择 choose their own courses：
(1) 学生自己选择会更有动力去学习。
Students will be more motivated to learn if they choose for themselves.
(2) 教授没办法了解每个学生的能力。
Professor cannot know every students' strength.

观点 I think students should choose their own courses.

论点 1：Firstly, students will be more motivated to learn those courses. For example, I

chose a course about how to use chemical elements to make healthy make-up. I was quite interested in this course and I spent extra time in the lab to test the different components. Not only did I get a good score，but also I learned a lot from it.

论点 2：Secondly，the professor cannot know every student's strengths. To be more specific，the professor could not choose the most suitable classes for students based on their personal interests and career goals.

3 Some universities require the students to choose a major field of study when they enter the school，while other universities require the students to learn several fields at first and then choose a major field of study. Which do you prefer? Why or why not?

选择 learn several fields at first and then choose major later：

(1) 学生能更好地了解自己的兴趣。

Students can better figure out their true passion.

(2) 学生上不同的课能认识更多朋友。

Student can make more friends by taking different classes.

观点 I would prefer to learn several fields at first and then choose my major field of study.

论点 1：Firstly，we can better figure out what our true passion is and decide on our major. For example，after my cousin took courses in medicine，business management，law and philosophy，he was really interested in law and wanted to protect people. So he decided to major in law. Now，he is a very successful lawyer.

论点 2：Secondly，I can make more friends if I take different courses. I mean，I can communicate with people from different professions and learn diverse knowledge from them. Probably we could become good friends and share some information.

五、历年真题题库

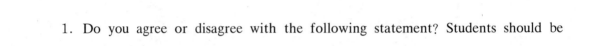

1. Do you agree or disagree with the following statement? Students should be allowed to take additional courses to graduate as soon as possible.

2. Do you agree or disagree with the following statement? People should always do what they are good at.

3. Which teacher's courses would you like to take? Why? Use specific reasons and examples to explain your choice.
   （1）A teacher who is humorous in class.
   （2）A teacher who is serious in class.

4. Some people think students should learn math when they study in colleges，while others think only those student who need it in the future should learn math in colleges. Which one do you prefer and why?

5. Do you agree or disagree with the following statement? Art and music students should also learn math and science classes. Use details and examples to support your opinion.

6. When students are reading，some choose the books from the reading list their

schools give. Others choose books by themselves. Which do you prefer?

7. Should parents discourage children from choosing some majors which might be very competitive to find a job in the future?

8. Some people think college students should learn specific courses like teaching or engineering. Others think they should learn general courses. Which do you prefer?

第二章　学校活动

一、核心话题真题

Do you agree or disagree with the following statement? All students should attend social activities such as join a club or a sports team in school.

【话题解析】

学校活动类话题是学习相关场景比较重要的一个类别,而美国大学也很鼓励同学们丰富课外生活,所以这类内容也和同学们之后的留学生活息息相关。此类话题在口语中出现的频率较高,相关的语料素材需要好好掌握。

这道题是典型的关于社团活动的选择。常见的变形题有:学生是否应该参加社团、社团的选择、课后选择学习还是社团活动等。除了社团活动外,还有一些题目是关于课外活动的,如学生是否应该参加课外活动、学生应该选择怎样的活动等。对于这类题目,我们回答的方向有以下几点:

(1)放松心情。

unwind oneself/recharge battery/release pressure

(2)帮助社交。

know new people/enlarge someone's social network

(3)学习技能。

pick up skills/catch up credits

（4）培养兴趣。

cultivate a hobby/form a habit/develop interest or talent

（5）求职加分。

successful in job-hunting/a plus in seeking for job opportunity/shing point in resume

二、核心词汇语料

obesity /əʊ'biːsəti/　*n*. 肥胖

recharge /riː'tʃɑːdʒ/　*v*. 恢复精力

benefit /'benɪfɪt/　*v*. 利于

vacation /veɪ'keɪʃn/　*n*. 假期

explore /ɪk'splɔːr/　*v*. 探索

relaxation /ˌriːlæk'seɪʃn/　*n*. 消遣

entertainment /ˌentər'teɪnmənt/　*n*. 娱乐

ease one's mind　放松

renewed energy　新的能量

build body strength　强健体魄

depressive disorder　抑郁症

social-developed　发展社交的

have access to information　获得信息

internship and job opportunities　实习和工作机会

sense of achievement　成就感

extra curricular activities　课外活动

be busy with　忙于

release the pressure　减轻压力

shift focus to   转移注意力

get refreshed   放松

develop interest   培养兴趣

explore new culture   探索新的文化

enlarge social network   扩大社交圈

mentally beneficial   有益心理健康

commercial use   商业用途

advancing technology   高科技

enjoyable experience   愉快的经历

三、满分回答 Sample

Do you agree or disagree with the following statement? All students should attend social activities such as join a club or a sports team in school.

观点 Personally，I agree with this statement.

论点 1：Firstly，attending club activities provides students an opportunity to meet others sharing the same goals and interest. They can even get information and resources which will support their current and future life. From personal experiences，I have met some of my best friends from my extra curricular activities and had many new doors open up to me.

论点 2：And also，it helps release the stress. Because students are always busy with all the schoolwork，they need to shift their focus to something else. So that they might

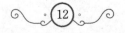

get refreshed and can be back to their classes with renewed energy.

四、变形题思路解析

1 Some college students take classes during the summer. Others take the summer off from school，so that they can rest or work. Which do you think is better for students? Explain why.

选择 take the summer off from school：

（1）学生暑假离校能放松身心。

Students taking the summer off from school can unwind themselves.

（2）充实的假期经历给他们的生活增添色彩。

The fulfilling experience outside of campus can add color to students' lives.

观点 Personally speaking，I'll definitely go with the second one.

论点 1：Firstly，we can unwind ourselves. To be more specific，summer break for schools means an extended breather that will recharge our bodies and minds. We can spend some quality time with our family and friends，and release the pressure from previous study，which will definitely be mentally beneficial.

论点 2：On top of that，the fulfilling experience outside of campus can benefit more to students. That's to say，summer vacation gives the students an opportunity to visit new places，increase their general knowledge，learn to explore new culture and develop their

own interests. These experiences would add colors to students' lives.

2 Do you agree or disagree with the following statement? Children should learn to draw or paint?

选择 agree：

(1) 孩子需要有一项爱好来享受生活。

Children need to have a hobby for enjoyment.

(2) 孩子能发展他们在艺术方面的特殊才能。

Children can develop their special talent about art.

观点 Personally speaking，I totally agree with the statement.

论点 1：Firstly，I think that children need to have a hobby for enjoyment. To be more specific，today's kids have much study to do and lots of mental stress. When they paint or draw，they can forget these stressful things and just enjoy the excitement and happiness during this solitary undisturbed process，which is definitely a good way to unwind themselves.

论点 2：On the other hand，children can develop their special talent about art. To be more specific，art helps children discover the joy of creating，and their interest would subconsciously guide them to explore more about the artistic world，so gradually they form a habit of creating，their imagination were boosted as well，it will ultimately be beneficial to them in their future career choice.

3 Which do you prefer when you were a child，playing indoors or outdoors?

选择 playing outdoors：

（1）户外活动直接关系到孩子的体力、体重和免疫功能，从而增强他们的健康。

Outdoor play is directly related to a child's physical strength，weight and immune function，so as to enhance their health.

（2）户外活动可以扩大孩子的社交圈，认识新朋友。

Outdoor games can enlarge children's social network and make new friends.

观点 Personally speaking，I'll definitely go with the second one.

论点 1：Firstly，outdoor play is directly related to a child's physical strength，weight and immune function，so as to enhance their health. To be more specific, playing outside allows kids to develop more advanced motor skills than children who spend most of their time indoors, since they need to walk，play and swing，their muscle strength would be improved as well.

论点 2：On the other hand，outdoor games can enlarge one's social network. That's to say，people will meet friends sharing common hobbies. Like my cousin who is one of those introversive teenagers，he does not like to speak in his school. However，after he attended an outdoor beach volleyball club，where he has regular activities every week，ever since then，he became a more active and socialized person with his members in his team.

4 Do you agree or disagree with the following statement? Children should begin watching news as a young age.

选择 agree：

（1）孩子可以学习各种科目，积累词汇。

Children could learn about a variety of subjects and accumulate vocabularies.

（2）孩子有更多话题与朋友讨论以维持友谊。

Children could share more news with their friends to maintain friendship.

观点 Personally speaking, I totally agree with the statement.

论点 1：Firstly, watching news can spark kids' learning about a variety of subjects. For instance, my 5-year-old cousin is a big fan of news, from where he was fascinated by the latest general events and also accumulated abundant of vocabularies from different coverage. In this way, kids are able to see how fun learning news can be and establish a habit of finding out more when things interest them.

论点 2：In addition, they can get latest knowledge to discuss with their friends, which is definitely a plus for maintaining friendship. To be more specific, the new topics can be held for discussion with their classmates, by exchanging ideas and feeling, they will know each other better.

5 Do you agree or disagree with the following statement? Parents should discourage children to join some competitive activities, like sports or entertainment.

选择 disagree：

（1）参加一些竞技活动能让孩子学习新技能，他们会在成年后很好地使用它们。

Joining some competitive activities can help children develop important skills, they'll use them well into adulthood.

（2）这会减少孩子交到新朋友的机会，因为孩子可以在这些活动中遇到其他有相同兴趣的孩子。

Discouraging would reduce children's chances to know new friends since children can meet other children with common interests during those activities.

观点　Personally speaking，I disagree with the statement.

论点 1：Firstly，joining competitive activities can help children develop important skills，they'll use them well into adulthood. For example，competition helps children learn that it is not always the best or the brightest who are successful，but rather those that work hard and stick with it，which would be a great way to inspire them to work harder.

论点 2：In addition，discouraging would reduce their chances to know new friends since children can meet other children with common interests during those activities. To be more specific，they have more chances to meet new people who are doing exact the same thing as they do，not only won't they feel alone about practicing，but also they can earn critical social skills through interacting with other children.

6　Do you agree or disagree with the following statement? Organizing team sports will help children become more social-developed.

选择 agree：

（1）团队运动能帮助孩子掌握沟通技巧并与他人合作。

Team sports can help children master communication skills and cooperate with others.

（2）孩子的情绪往往更加稳定，在面对压力时能够让自己冷静下来。

Children tend to be more emotionally stable and able to calm themselves down when react to pressure.

观点 Personally speaking, I agree with the statement.

论点 1：Firstly，team sports can help children master communication skills and cooperate with others. For example，baseball is a popular team sport，which involves two teams of nine starting players，each member of the team must have a unique skill set to be effective，so the team as a whole can reach its goal to win the game. Children will inevitably need to share their ideas and discuss strategies，which makes them feel the sense of belonging to a social group rather than fighting alone as individuals.

论点 2：On top of that，children tend to be more emotionally stable and able to calm themselves down when react to pressure. To be more specific，in team sports，children need to act quickly and make split-second decisions that could prove to be a win or a loss，and that decisions usually come with a tremendous amount of pressure. Needless to say，the ability to handle pressure can be especially useful when making those same types of decisions in their later life.

7 Some secondary schools require that every student's schedule include a study hall，which is a free class period during the school day in which students can do class assignments or rest. Do you think this is a good idea? Why or why not? Use details and examples in your response.

选择 agree：

（1）利用这段时间帮助学生弥补他们在课堂上没有掌握的一些重要知识点。

Use this time period to help students to make up for some important information they don't fully grasp in class.

（2）学生能更高效地完成作业。

Students might finish their assignments more efficiently.

观点 Personally speaking，I agree with the statement.

论点 1：Firstly，this can help students to make up for some important information they don't fully grasp in class. To be more specific，some kids may be distracted so they might miss a bunch of essential points during class. Therefore，they can make use of this period to discuss with their classmates，either checking on their notes or ask each other directly，so as to make up for the loss，which is substantial in the long-term learning.

论点 2：In addition，students might finish their assignments more efficiently. That is to say，students usually may be disrupted doing their homework at home，either by the conversation from their parents asking them to have dinner or the notifications from their phones. So in this way，they can get out of their comfort zone to be more productive，instead of wasting time doing nothing in their own bedrooms，they will utilize this time to finish their homework as soon as possible and then go home free to enjoy their after school time at ease.

五、历年真题题库

1. Do you agree or disagree with the following statement? Children shouldn't watch

TV news or listen to radio when they are very young.

2. Do you agree or disagree with the following statement? Children can learn valuable things from playing video games?

3. Do you think it is a good idea for children to keep pets?

4. Some college students like to join clubs and enjoy club activities, others like to spend their time studying another courses or doing school work. Which do you think is better?

5. Some people think that those children who do not want to keep learning a musical instrument course should be required to keep learning the course; while others think that those children should be allowed to make decisions by themselves (they can still do exercises by themselves). What is your opinion and why? Use examples and details in your explanation.

6. Do you agree or disagree with the following statement? Young people should learn to draw or paint.

7. Your university plans to reduce expenditure recently, which clubs do you think the university should stop funding? Sports clubs like skiing club, or academic clubs like math club. Please give reasons and details in your answer.

第三章　勤 工 俭 学

一、核心话题真题

Do you agree or disagree with the following statement? School should limit the time that student doing part-time jobs in school.

【话题解析】

勤工俭学是许多人在大学生涯中都会体验的一段经历,这个话题在托福口语考试中不是很常见,但是也会考到,而我们在回答一些其他口语题的时候很可能会碰到这个话题。而对于很多还没有经历大学生活的同学们来说,这个话题相对陌生一些。因此对于这类话题我们可以通过以下几个方面来回答:

(1) 赚钱。

earn more money/financial independence/ease financial pressure

(2) 认识新朋友。

know new people/enlarge one's social network

(3) 学习技能。

pick up useful skills

(4) 积累经验。

accumulate working experiences

(5) 求职加分。

a plus in seeking for job opportunities/shining point in resume

(6) 培养兴趣。

develop interests

二、核心词汇语料

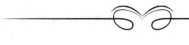

refreshed /rɪˈfreʃt/ *adj*. 恢复活力的

challenging /ˈtʃælɪndʒɪŋ/ *adj*. 富有挑战性的

colleague /ˈkɒliːg/ *n*. 同事

distract /dɪˈstrækt/ *v*. 分心

introvert /ˈɪntrəvɜːt/ *n*. 性格内向的人

internship /ˈɪntɜːnʃɪp/ *n*. 实习

graduation /ˌgrædʒuˈeɪʃn/ *n*. 毕业

degree /dɪˈgriː/ *n*. 学位

mental health 心理健康

lower-risk 低风险

a great deal 很多

off the clock 下班

social interaction 社交

evening shift 晚班

less pressure 更小的压力

figure out 解决

work experience 工作经验

job-hunting 求职

zone out 发呆

gap year　间隔年

perform monotonous tasks　执行单调的任务

a waste of time and energy　浪费时间和精力

prioritize one's studies　把学习放在首位

三、满分回答 Sample

Do you agree or disagree with the following statement? School should limit the time that student doing part-time jobs in school.

观点 Personally speaking, I disagree with the statement.

论点 1：First of all, it is essential for students to ease financial pressure. To be more specific, students never have enough money to sustain themselves, not to mention those who need to support their families. Preparing gifts for my relatives or myself by extra money I earned comes with amazing feelings of adulthood and pride.

论点 2：Second of all, students can gain some important experiences from doing part-time jobs. For example, if students do manage to find a job that's relevant to their major, they'll be able to practice the knowledge they receive in class immediately. And even if they don't get the job in a relevant field, they will still gain a lot of soft and hard skills.

四、变形题思路解析

1 Some people think it's better to take classes in the daytime and have a part-time job in the evening, some people prefer to have a part-time job in the daytime and take classes in the evening. Which do you think is better?

选择 take classes in the daytime：

（1）白天上课更高效。

It's more efficient to take classes in the daytime.

（2）晚上通常工作压力更小。

Working evening shift usually comes with less pressure.

观点 Personally speaking, I will prefer the first choice.

论点 1：Firstly, It's more efficient to take classes in the daytime. To be more specific, after a whole night's sleep, we have completely recharged our battery for the next day, and our mind would be refreshed to prepare for any challenging tasks that required a great deal of thinking. So we will be productive and effective to focus on studying.

论点 2：Apart from that, working evening shift usually comes with less pressure. That's to say, during the night when most of the staff are off the clock, our social interaction will be super limited. There's no one to boss us around and we almost have no colleagues to distract us. Less pressure means it is good for our mental health especially for an introvert like me.

2 Do you agree or disagree with the following statement? Students should work for a year before entering university.

选择 agree：

(1) 给学生充足的时间想清楚选什么专业。

It can give students enough time to think about what major to choose.

(2) 这是一条增加工作经验方便毕业后找工作的好途径。

It's a wonderful way to obtain work experiences for job-hunting after graduation.

观点 Personally speaking, I totally agree with the statement.

论点 1：Firstly, a gap year will give students the time to think about what major to choose, and what they should go to school for. For example, there are so many students without clearly figuring out their true interests, such situation actually happens a lot even after enrollment. Not only is it costly, but also it is a waste of time.

论点 2：On top of that, this is a wonderful way to obtain work experiences for job-hunting after graduation. To be more specific, employers would be more likely to hire applicants with sufficient working experiences than who only hold degrees. It provides students with more hands-on skills to know how to take actions, not just following the textbooks as a green hand.

五、历年真题题库

Do you agree or disagree with the following statement? School should limit the time that student doing part-time jobs in school.

第四章　学分与考试

一、核心话题真题

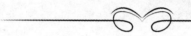

Do you agree or disagree with the following statement? Students should be allowed to take additional courses to graduate as soon as possible.

【话题解析】

在大学里,学分与考试是和同学们的生活息息相关的话题,而这类话题的题目及其变形题,在最近三年的托福口语独立题中是比较常出现的。这种题目比较简单,但是对于许多没有大学经历的同学来说有些陌生,比如这道题关于"学生是否应该被允许选修额外的课程,以便早点毕业"。其实在大学校园中有许多同学确实如此选择,因此对于这类话题我们可以通过事实情况来作出选择。对于这类话题我们整理了如下"万能"方向,可以运用到相应的题目中:

(1) 压力太大。

stress out/too much pressure

(2) 增加工作量。

add workload

(3) 激发学生兴趣。

stimulate students' interests in ...

(4) 提高学习效率。

improve the efficiency of study

二、核心词汇语料

interest /ˈɪntrəst/　*n*. 兴趣

elective /ɪˈlektɪv/　*n*. 选修课

nightmare /ˈnaɪtmeə(r)/　*n*. 噩梦

credit /ˈkredɪt/　*n*. 学分

inspire /ɪnˈspaɪər/　*v*. 激发；鼓舞

perform /pərˈfɔːrm/　*v*. 表现

seminar /ˈsemɪnɑːr/　*n*. 研讨班

utilize /ˈjuːtəlaɪz/　*v*. 利用；使用

apply to　应用到

real-life situations　真实生活场景

pay attention to class　认真上课

have motivation　有动力

eager to　热衷于

be put under pressure　承受压力

discover one's talents　发现自己的才华

explore fields of interests　探索感兴趣的领域

follow one's heart　跟随自己的内心

become annoyed　感到厌烦

have a negative attitude　有负面情绪

negative effect　负面效果

mental health　心理健康

excel at　擅长于

pay back　偿还

enhance skills　提高技能

gain a wealth of knowledge　获得丰富的知识

get distracted　分心

student loans　学生贷款

三、满分回答 Sample

Do you agree or disagree with the following statement? Students should be allowed to take additional courses to graduate as soon as possible.

观点 Personally speaking，I do think schools should allow students to do that.

论点 1： First of all，some students are capable of doing that without being stressed out. Take myself as an example，when I was at college，I took twenty-two credits during my freshman year，which was more than the suggested sixteen credits. However，I did manage to have everything under control，and I don't think there's any downside of doing it.

论点 2： Second of all，some people might need to graduate as soon as possible and get to work because they have to pay back their student loans. The cost for four years seems too much of a burden，so they will try to find a job as soon as possible. That should be allowed.

四、变形题思路解析

1 Do you think the school should let two teachers take turns to teach one class?

选择 not a good idea：

（1）这会给老师增加工作量。

It would add workload to teachers.

（2）学生有时会感到困惑。

Students can get confused sometimes.

观点 Personally speaking，I don't think it's a good idea for two teachers to take turns.

论点 1：First of all，it would add workload to teachers. Teachers will now have to communicate before classes for they want to avoid repeating chapters. And they also need to know how every student is performing in the other class，which can take a lot of time.

论点 2：Second of all，students can get confused sometimes. Take myself as an example，when I was a freshman，one of my classes was taught by two professors in turns. Sometimes they approach things in different ways and explain concepts from different perspectives. It can get really perplexing.

2 Do you agree or disagree with the school policy that in order to improve the writing skills, all first-year students should be required to take writing courses which involve writing several essays as a requirement?

选择 agree：

(1) 写作课可以提升学生的写作兴趣。

Writing courses can raise students' interests in writing.

(2) 学生需要老师帮忙纠正他们的错误。

Students need teachers to correct their mistakes.

观点 Personally speaking, I do think it's a great idea.

论点 1：First of all, writing courses can raise students' interests in writing. Take my little brother as an example, when he came back from his writing class, he was so excited about the things they talked about in class, the plays they watched, the picture books they read. Thanks to the teacher, we can see his growing interest in creating some passages and writing diaries.

论点 2：Second of all, students need teachers to correct their mistakes. Family members might not be the best people to educate children regarding their school work. For example, our mom can get pretty upset when she was correcting the essay for my little brother, which is definitely not good.

3 In order to improve students' grade, do you think the university should give students a lot of homework?

选择 I don't think so：

（1）这让学生有压力。

It stresses students out.

（2）更好的方式是激励学生。

The best way to learn is to inspire students.

观点 Personally speaking，I don't think it's a good way to improve grade.

论点 1：First of all，it stresses students out. I remember when I was in high school，we had so much homework every day that nobody ever finished them before ten o'clock at night. We were so tired that we were falling asleep easily in the morning classes，we also got distracted easily because we didn't get enough sleep.

论点 2：Second of all，the best way to learn is to inspire students. Take my physics teacher as an example，he did a lot of fun stuff in the class and that really raised our interests in the subject. He would do inspiring experiments in front of us，and he also showed us the videos about exploring the universe.

4 Your university is planning to require all first-year students to take a class that they would learn how to use the resources available at the university library and apply those skills in writing a long research paper. Do you think this is a good idea?

选择 I think it's a good idea：

（1）很多学生不知道如何利用现有的资料。

Many students have no idea how to use the available resources.

（2）这些技能在大学时期非常重要。

These skills are helpful throughout college.

观点 Personally speaking, I do think it's a great idea.

论点 1: First of all, most students have no idea how to use the available resources. Take myself as an example, when I just entered college, I took a seminar showing us how to do all those things in the library. It was a lot different than high school, so it would be hard for freshmen to know how to utilize all these resources on their own.

论点 2: Second of all, these skills are helpful throughout college. During the four years of my college, there were a lot of classes that require essay or paper as an assignment. And I have been using the library website all the time to search for books and refer to information. This is really an indispensable part of college life.

5 Which do you prefer? An interesting class but very strict with scoring, or a boring class that gives you high scores.

选择 an interesting class：

(1) 有趣的课堂可以激发学生兴趣。

An interesting class might inspire students.

(2) 无聊的课堂对学习无益。

A boring class isn't really helpful with learning.

观点 Personally speaking, I would like an interesting class but very strict with scoring.

论点 1：First of all，interesting class might inspire students. Take my math teacher as an example，he added a lot of interesting elements to the class to attract our attention，not only does it make us more receptive to knowledge，but it also makes us more interested in math.

论点 2：Second of all，a boring class that gives high score isn't really helpful with learning. I remember having this one mechanical engineering class in junior. The professor was just reading from slides and the class was really bad. Though I got an A minus for that class，I learnt nothing.

五、历年真题题库

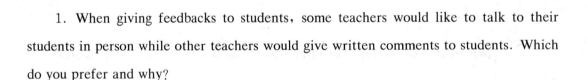

1. When giving feedbacks to students，some teachers would like to talk to their students in person while other teachers would give written comments to students. Which do you prefer and why?

2. Which one do you prefer? Review your notes after class and keep doing this throughout the whole semester or just review at the end of the semester?

3. Do you agree with the idea of recording the lecture and uploading it on the website?

4. Do you agree or disagree with the following statement? A school should no more require students to do experiments but show students the videos of experiments. Why? Please give reasons and examples to support your response.

5. Do you agree or disagree that students would learn more if the teachers assign them with more schoolwork?

6. Some professors prefer to answer students' questions in the end of the lecture, and others stop at different points to answer students' questions. Which style do you think is better for learning?

7. Do you agree or disagree with the following statement? It is okay for professors to forbid students to record lectures.

8. Do you agree or disagree with the following statement? Teachers should give awards to students who get good grades in order to increase the competition in class.

第五章　工作关系

一、核心话题真题

Some managers tend to check worker's task closely or frequently，while others tend to check them rarely or causally. Which is better for the management?

【话题解析】

工作关系也是托福口语考试中常出现的一类题型,然而这个话题对于很多同学来说相对陌生,他们在平时的生活中也没有太多对于工作方面的思考。甚至有一部分同学在回答这类题的时候,语言表达相对比较空洞,内容脱离现实。

工作相关的话题,通常会对工作环境,如大公司或小公司;薪酬待遇,如高薪或低薪;工作氛围,如有无领导管制等内容进行考查。对于此类话题我们可以从以下几个角度进行思考:

(1)时间。

working efficiency/time-efficient/time-consuming

(2)金钱。

earn more money/be financially stable

(3)放松。

drive me overwhelmed/ease my burden/develop mutual trust

（4）环境。

motivational working atmosphere

（5）个人发展。

get promoted/develop innovative ideas

二、核心词汇语料

innovative /ˈɪnəveɪtɪv/　*adj.* 创新的

efficiency /ɪˈfɪʃnsi/　*n.* 效率

enhance /ɪnˈhæns/　*v.* 加强

supervision /ˌsuːpəˈvɪʒn/　*n.* 监督

overwhelmed /ˌoʊvərˈwelmd/　*adj.* 被压垮的

procrastination /prəʊˌkræstɪˈneɪʃ(ə)n/　*n.* 拖延

authoritative /əˈθɔːrəteɪtɪv/　*adj.* 权威性的；命令式的

creative /kriˈeɪtɪv/　*adj.* 创造的

space /speɪs/　*n.* 空间

unreliable /ˌʌnrɪˈlaɪəbl/　*adj.* 不可靠的

unequal /ʌnˈiːkwəl/　*adj.* 不平等的

unconsciously procrastinate　无意识地拖延

slack off　偷懒

swipe one's cellphone　刷手机

short clips　短视频

copy and follow the behavior　学习模仿行为

chat with sb.　与某人交谈

fix the problem　解决问题

in vain　徒劳

move on　　向前

in a close contact　　密切联系

get promoted　　升职

motivational working atmosphere　　激励的工作氛围

long-term development　　长期的发展

三、满分回答 Sample

Some managers tend to check worker's task closely or frequently，while others tend to check them rarely or causally. Which is better for the management?

观点　Personally speaking，I think it is better to check worker's tasks closely.

论点 1：First of all，it could enhance their working efficiency. For example，some employees might unconsciously procrastinate or slack off during work，like swiping their cellphones，watching some short clips，and chatting with their friends. They definitely need such supervision to focus more on their tasks.

论点 2：Besides，it would also create a motivational working atmosphere. Let's say，when employees confront some challenges in their tasks，they are likely to feel confused and even overwhelmed. At this point，managers would notice their issues in time，and give some guidance and encouraging words to cheer them up. So employees could stay energized and motivated.

四、变形题思路解析

1 Some managers like to closely watch their employees, while others prefer to give them more freedom. Which do you think is more effective?

选择 give employees more freedom：

（1）紧密查看可能会使员工有压力。

Watching closely might drive employees overwhelmed.

（2）自由度可以让员工更好地创新。

Freedom could help employees to innovate better.

观点 As for me, I prefer to give employees more freedom.

论点 1: At first, watching closely might drive employees overwhelmed. For example, my brother Peter used to finish the tasks quietly on his own. In this case, his manager's frequent check sounds kind of authoritative and pushy to him, and he doesn't feel the mutual trust. In return, such monitoring stresses him out to a larger extent.

论点 2: In addition, freedom could help employees to innovate better. To be more specific, during self-exploration, employees could freely develop their minds and delve into their work. It is more likely to come up with new methods and ideas in their working projects. So freedom could open more space for them to be creative.

2 Some people like to work independently and enjoy more freedom，while others like to have a supervisor to tell them what to do. Which do you prefer? Why?

选择 have a supervisor：

(1) 这能提高员工的工作效率。

It can enhance employees' working efficiency.

(2) 这能创造一种激励人心的工作氛围。

It would create a motivational working atmosphere.

观点 Personally speaking，I think it is better to have a supervisor.

论点 1：First of all，it could enhance employees' working efficiency. For example，some employees might unconsciously procrastinate or slack off during work，like swiping their cellphones，watching some short clips，and chatting with their friends. They definitely need such supervision to focus more on their tasks.

论点 2：Besides，it would create a motivational working atmosphere. Let's say，when employees confront some challenges in their tasks，they are likely to feel confused and even overwhelmed. At this point，managers would notice their issues in time，and give some guidance and encouraging words to cheer them up. So employees could stay energized and motivated.

3 Do you agree or disagree with the following statement? Boss should maintain close relationship with employees.

选择 agree：

(1) 这能提高员工的工作积极性。

It can enhance employees' working motivation.

(2) 这有促进相互信任的作用。

It also functions to promote mutual trust.

观点 Honestly, I agree with this statement that boss should maintain close relationship with employees.

论点 1: Firstly, for bosses, it helps their employees work more motivated. For instance, when employees meet challenges in their working tasks, in close contact, bosses could directly sense their change and give them some suggestions to fix the problem. It is beneficial to prevent employees' procrastination.

论点 2: Plus, for employees, it also functions to promote mutual trust. Take myself as an example, my manager and I are intimate friends both in work and life. It is enjoyable for me to share my thoughts, discuss some interesting news, and even go to the gym together with her. I feel like I am equally respected and trusted without push or judgment.

4 Do you agree or disagree with the following statement? It is acceptable that someone use other's influence to get a job.

选择 disagree：

(1) 这会削弱其他应聘者的信心。

It would weaken other applicants' confidence.

(2) 这可能会形成一个不公平的工作环境。

It might shape an unequal working atmosphere.

观点 From my perspective, I totally disagree with the statement.

论点 1: First of all, it would weaken other applicants' confidence. For instance, my sister Jenny complains to me that her coworker easily gets a better job only due to her relatives in the company. Such situation puts her efforts and determination in vain, and she feels really hurtful to move on.

论点 2: Moreover, it might shape an unequal working atmosphere. Let's say, if one person gets the job so easily by relationship, the others in the company would copy and follow such behavior to get promoted quickly. To this end, everyone would not make effort to their work, but flatter their managers, which would be a shame for the whole company's reputation.

5 Imagine a company has hired you as an employee and offered a very high salary. However, the company is controversial regarding what it's doing to earn money and receives negative criticism from people. Would you accept this job?

选择 not accept：

(1) 这份工作让我承担很多压力。

It would drive me extremely overwhelmed.

(2) 这不利于自身长远发展。

It is not beneficial for long-term development.

观点 Frankly, I would not accept this job.

论点 1: To begin with, it would drive me extremely overwhelmed. To be more specific, as a high-salary taker, I definitely need to stand out and advertise for the company in public. And the audience would not give me a favorable look and even spit me some curse words as they think I am a liar. It strains me so much to see my image as unreliable.

论点 2: On top of that, it is not beneficial for long-term development. I should think about what kind of work the company is truly doing, it is possible that they are doing something illegal like smuggling drugs and kidnapping children or females, not to mention gangster fights. I don't want to throw myself in more upcoming troubles.

五、历年真题题库

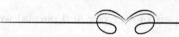

1. Do you agree or disagree with the following statement? It is acceptable that someone use other's influence to get a job.

2. Imagine a company has hired you as an employee and offered a very high salary. However, the company is controversial regarding what it's doing to earn money and receives negative criticism from people. Would you accept this job?

第六章 时间安排

一、核心话题真题

Some people choose jobs with higher pay but little vacation time（need to work on weekends），while others choose jobs with lower pay and normal work schedule. Which one do you prefer and why?

【话题解析】

在工作类话题中,时间安排类题目的出现频率也比较高。对于还没有工作经验的同学们来说,大家可以联想自己在学习中是怎么安排时间的。这道题的意思是:"有些人喜欢高薪但假期很少的工作(需要周末工作),而有一些人喜欢工资不高但有正常工作时间的工作。"如果我们选择后者,那么可以总结出以下"万能"论点:

(1) 让我放松。

make me relaxed

(2) 对心理健康有好处。

good for mental health

(3) 更加有效率。

more productive

二、核心词汇语料

occupation /ˌɑːkjuˈpeɪʃn/　*n*. 工作

profession /prəˈfeʃn/　*n*. 职业

dedicated /ˈdedɪˌkeɪtɪd/　*adj*. 努力认真的

salary /ˈsæləri/　*n*. 工资

welfare /ˈwelfer/　*n*. 福利

unemployed /ˌʌnɪmˈplɔɪd/　*adj*. 无业的

demanding /dɪˈmændɪŋ/　*adj*. 要求高的

stressful /ˈstresfl/　*adj*. 有压力的

steady /ˈstedi/　*adj*. 稳定的

repetitive /rɪˈpetətɪv/　*adj*. 反复的

tiring /ˈtaɪərɪŋ/　*adj*. 累人的

exhausting /ɪɡˈzɔːstɪŋ/　*adj*. 令人精疲力竭的

resume /rɪˈzuːm/　*n*. 简历

workload /ˈwɜːkləʊd/　*n*. 工作量

coworker /ˈkəʊ wɜːrkər/　*n*. 同事

bonus /ˈbəʊnəs/　*n*. 奖金

salary /ˈsæləri/　*n*. 收入

client /ˈklaɪənt/　*n*. 顾客

freelancer /ˈfriːlænsər/　*n*. 自由职业

chill /tʃɪl/　*n*. 放松

workaholic /wɜːkəˈhɒlɪk/　*n*. 工作狂

be burned out　累得筋疲力尽

human resources　人力资源

be on guard　处于警惕状态

be snowed under　有太多工作要做

benefit future development　惠及未来发展

routine work　常规工作

work overtime/extra hours　加班

part-time　兼职,打零工

give me a sense of accomplishment　给我一种成就感

put my talent into full play　充分发挥我的天赋

三、满分回答 Sample

Some people choose jobs with higher pay but little vacation time（need to work on weekends）, while others choose jobs with lower pay and normal work schedule. Which one do you prefer and why?

观点 I prefer jobs with lower pay and normal work schedule.

论点 1: First of all, It can make me relaxed, which is good for my mental health. For instance, in my last job, I got paid a lot but I was asked to work overtime constantly. Even when I was off work, I still checked my work emails a lot just in case there were some extra projects that needed my attention. My mental health was affected and I was so stressed that I had to quit the job.

论点 2: Second, I can be more productive when I have a normal work schedule. To be more specific, with a normal work schedule, I can have enough rest time. With enough rest，I will be able to concentrate on work better during work time and be more productive.

四、变形题思路解析

1 When people are working, some prefer to do hard work first and then do easy work，while others want to do the easy work first and then do the hard one. Which way do you prefer?

选择 do easy work first：

（1）先做简单的工作让我觉得更有效率。

Getting the easy work done first will make me feel more productive.

（2）我能更快进入工作状态。

I will be able to enter the state of work faster.

观点 I prefer to do the easy work first.

论点 1：First，it will make me feel more productive. For example，last weekend，I was doing my schoolwork. I chose to do the math exercise first which I was good at. I only spent half an hour to finish it and I felt really efficient and confident about the rest of the work.

论点 2：Second，I will be able to enter the state of the work faster. To be more specific，my brain can think step by step，warming up from some simple questions and then thinking about some complex ones.

2 Some companies have recently started to give their employees more extra time to socialize or do non-work activities during the workday. The theory is that this will increase productivity. Do you agree or disagree?

选择 agree：

(1) 这可以让我更放松，有益心理健康。

It can make me more relaxed and it is good for my mental health.

(2) 我将更加了解同事，可以与他们很好地一起工作。

I will get to know my coworkers better and we can work well together.

观点 I agree with the plan that companies started to give their employees more extra time to socialize or do non-work activities during the workday for the following reasons.

论点 1：Firstly, it can make me more relaxed and good for my mental health. For example, I used to be an intern at an IT company. The manager there gave us two free afternoons. I used the free time to exercise or socialize with my friends. So I always felt chill and pleasant at work.

论点 2：Secondly, I will get to know my coworkers better and we can work well together. I mean, we could communicate more during the free time and find some common interests or topics. Probably, we could become good friends.

3 Do you agree or disagree with the following statement? Employees should be allowed to read personal mail and text messages at work time.

选择 disagree：

(1) 这会降低员工的工作效率。

This will lower the working efficiency of the worker.

(2) 它们可以用电话代替。

They can use phone calls instead.

观点 I don't agree that employees should be allowed to read personal mail and text messages during work time.

论点 1：First，this will lower the working efficiency of the workers. To be more specific，some workers will be distracted reading their personal email or text messages that they cannot focus on their work well. For example，in my dad's company，the employees are allowed to do this. When I went to visit his company，I saw the workers on their phone，slacking off for a long time. They were so inefficient.

论点 2：Second，if workers really need to deal with personal emergencies，they can use phone calls instead. I think that usually text messages and emails are not very urgent. Like if there's a medical emergency that the worker needs to attend to in his family，his family can always call him.

4 Do you prefer regular working hours or more free hours to work from home?

选择 work from home：

（1）我能节约通勤时间。

I can save time on the commute.

（2）我能节约通勤费用。

I can save money on commuting.

 I prefer to work from home.

论点1：Firstly，working at home will be more efficient. I mean，I may arrange my schedule to avoid the traffic jam in rush hours. However，if choosing the first one，in my city when everyone goes to work and gets off work at a certain time，the traffic will be very congested，I may spend two more hours than the normal time in commuting.

论点2：Secondly，this way may help me save money. For example，in my city，normally I may only spend around ten dollars by taxi in commuting fifteen kilometers. If I am caught by the traffic congestion，I may have to spend around twenty dollars by taxi in commuting for the same distance.

五、历年真题题库

1. Some people go to take exercise outside or go to gym each day，while others take exercise or go to gym when they have free time. Which opinion would you prefer? Please give your reasons.

2. Some people prefer to finish the assignment a long time before the due date while

others prefer finishing assignment right before the due date. Which one do you prefer?

3. Do you agree or disagree with the following statement? It's more important to spend time with family than to spend time simply on study or working.

4. Do you prefer to do different projects at the same time or only one project?

5. Imagine you are going to learn a course. Do you prefer a course that meets once a week and will be completed in a few months, or a course that meets several times a week and will be completed in a few weeks? Please explain why and use details to explain.

6. Should universities limit the time students are allowed to spend on part-time jobs on campus?

7. Some students like to have a break during weekends or summer vacation. Others think it is better to take a class. Which do you prefer and why?

8. Which do you prefer, a high pay job with longer working time or an average pay job with normal work time?

9. Some college students like to join clubs and enjoy club activities, others like to spend their time studying another courses or doing schoolwork. Which one do you think is better and why?

第七章　朋友关系

一、核心话题真题

Some people prefer to make friends with people who share similar ages while other people prefer to make friends with people from different age groups. Which one do you prefer? Why?

【话题解析】

朋友关系类型的题目，在托福口语考试独立题中出现得不算高频，但是问题比较多样化。因为比较抽象，所以这种题目会相对难一些。这道题的意思是："一些人喜欢和同龄人交朋友，一些人喜欢和不同年龄的人交朋友，你喜欢哪一种？"对于这道题，我们可以选择不同年龄的人。我们可以总结出以下"万能"论点：

(1) 从他们的生活经历中学习。

learn from their life experiences

(2) 请教他们生活中的问题。

ask them questions about difficulties in life

二、核心词汇语料

buddy /'bʌdi/　n. 伙伴

respect /rɪ'spekt/　n. 尊重

listener /'lɪsənər/　n. 倾听者

hug /hʌg/　n. 拥抱

sincere /sɪn'sɪr/　adj. 真诚的

lifelong /'laɪf'lɔŋ/　adj. 一辈子的

support /sə'pɔːrt/　n. 支持；v. 支持

bond /bɑːnd/　n. 情感联系

acquaintance /ə'kweɪntəns/　n. 相识

affectionate /ə'fekʃənət/　adj. 亲切的

amicable /'æmɪkəbl/　adj. 和蔼的

considerate /kən'sɪdərət/　adj. 考虑周到的

emotional /ɪ'məʊʃənl/　adj. 情绪化的

enthusiastic /ɪnˌθuːziˈæstɪk/　adj. 热情的

expressive /ɪk'spresɪv/　adj. 表现力强的

favorite /'feɪvərɪt/　adj. 最喜欢的

frank /fræŋk/　adj. 直白的

friendly /'frendli/　adj. 友好的

generous /'dʒenərəs/　adj. 大方的

gentle /'dʒentl/　adj. 温柔的

helpful /'helpfl/　adj. 有帮助的

honest /'ɑːnɪst/　adj. 诚实的

humorous /'hjuːmərəs/　adj. 幽默的

ideal /aɪˈdiːəl/   *adj*. 理想的

intimate /ˈɪntɪmət/   *adj*. 亲密的

kind /kaɪnd/   *adj*. 善良的

patient /ˈpeɪʃnt/   *adj*. 耐心的

reunion /ˌriːˈjuːniən/   *n*. 团聚

sociable /ˈsəʊʃəbl/   *adj*. 善于交际的

sympathetic /ˌsɪmpəˈθetɪk/   *adj*. 有同理心的

talkative /ˈtɔːkətɪv/   *adj*. 健谈的

thoughtful /ˈθɔːtfl/   *adj*. 周到的

trustworthy /ˈtrʌstwɜːrði/   *adj*. 值得信赖的

companion /kəmˈpæniən/   *n*. 伴侣

caring /ˈkɛrɪŋ/   *adj*. 照顾人的

hit it off   聊得来，投缘

get along with   和······合得来

hang out   一起玩

form a special rapport   建立特别的关系

mutual interests   共同的兴趣

三、满分回答 Sample

Some people prefer to make friends with people who share similar ages while other people prefer to make friends with people from different age groups. Which one do you prefer? Why?

观点 I prefer to make friends with people from different age groups.

论点 1：First，I can learn from my friends' life experiences. For example，I have a friend who is ten years older than me. He has already been through my stage of life. He was working as a computer programmer then he switched to teaching music，which is his true passion. I have learned from his experience to follow my true passion.

论点 2：Second，I can ask them questions if I meet difficulties in life. To be more specific，when I make friends who are older than me，I can ask them for their opinions on my life and follow their advice. For example，when I have questions about relationships，studying，or work，I always ask my older friends and they offer wise advice.

四、变形题思路解析

1 Which one of the two patterns would help people to know each other better，meeting at the first sight or through long-term relationship?

选择 through long-term relationship：

（1）第一印象可能不准确。

First impressions are not always accurate.

（2）有更多的经历让我们更好地了解对方。

Going through more experiences will help us know each other better.

观点 Well，personally，I think it is more advisable to get to know a person by

long time observation.

论点 1：First，I think first impressions might not be accurate. To be more specific，one might not be able to learn the real characteristics or personalities of that person on the first sight since the person might be a little shy and he or she might not behave in the way they normally do.

论点 2：Also，going through more experiences will help us know each other better. For example，I have known my best friend Jessie since kindergarten. Gradually，we found out that we were both interested in drawing and travelling when we were getting more familiar.

2 We should be completely honest and open with friends. Agree or disagree?

选择 disagree：

（1）有时候真相会伤害别人。

Sometimes truths can hurt others.

（2）人和人之间的距离很重要。

Personal distance between people is important.

观点 I disagree with the statement.

论点 1：First，sometimes truths can hurt others. For example，once my best friend Jessie wore a new dress. She was so excited and showed me the picture. But I thought the pattern of the dress was out of fashion，so I told her the truth. But I didn't think about her feelings. After hearing my words，she was very disappointed.

论点2: Second, personal distance between people is important. To be more specific, keeping proper distance is more comfortable for the social interaction. Everyone needs space and keeps their privacy.

3 Do you agree or disagree with the following statement? Friends can maintain friendship even if they have disagreements.

选择 agree:

(1) 人和人之间有不同的想法很正常。

It's normal for people to have different opinions.

(2) 我们只要价值观相同就可以做朋友。

We can stay friends as long as we have similar values.

观点 I totally agree with the following statement.

论点1: First of all, it's normal for people to have different opinions. For instance, my best friend Amanda and I once had a disagreement over how to spend our leisure time. She likes to watch movies and I thought it's a waste of time. I prefer to read books, which is boring to her. But we still maintain our friendship now.

论点2: Second, we can stay friends as long as we have similar values. To be more specific, if we are both willing to respect each other and are decent, kind people, then we can be friends.

4 Some people think that we don't have to accept gifts that we don't need, while others think we should accept the gifts even if we may never need them. Which one do you agree? Use details and examples in your answer.

选择 accept gifts even if we may never need them：

(1) 如果我们不接受礼物可能会伤害朋友。

We may hurt our friends if we don't accept the gift.

(2) 礼物是友谊的纪念。

Gifts are souvenirs of the friendships.

观点 I prefer to accept gifts even if we may never need them.

论点 1：First，if we refuse the gift，it may hurt others. For example，once my best friend Amy gave me a new CD as my birthday gift. She was so excited but I did not really like the band. So I told her that I was not a big fan of that band and she could keep the CD herself. However，she was really disappointed and upset.

论点 2：Second，gifts are souvenirs of friendships. I mean，the gift is a symbol of our friendship. It doesn't matter what exactly we receive，but what matters is that we have a good memory.

5 Do you agree or disagree with the statement that roommates must be good friends?

选择 disagree：

(1) 住在一起是为了省钱。

Living together is for saving money.

（2）成为好朋友很难。

It's difficult to make good friends.

观点 I disagree with the following statement that roommates must be good friends.

论点 1：First，living together is just for saving money. To be more specific，sharing a room with others allows us to share living expenses，such as rent and utilities. This can reduce our living burden，especially for international students，which is a significant expense.

论点 2：Secondly，to become friends，we need to share a same life style. For example，I used to have a roommate who loves to stay at home and plays video games while I like to travel around and communicate with others. We are too different to become good friends.

五、历年真题题库

1. Some people like surprise visits from their friends，others prefer to be informed ahead of the visit. Which one do you prefer and why?

2. Do you agree or disagree with the following statement? We should not try to help our friends unless they ask for help.

3. Do you agree that children should spend some time visiting their relatives or

friends? Explain why.

4. When you disagree with your friends and family on some controversial issues, would you choose to convince them or just keep the disagreements?

5. Some people like to make decision based on their own experience while other people prefer to ask others for help such as family and friends. Which do you prefer and why?

6. Do you agree or disagree with the following statement? We should be complete honest and open to our close friends. Explain why.

7. Some people prefer to make friends with people who share similar ages while other people prefer to make friends with people from different age groups. Which one do you agree? Why?

8. Some people prefer to stay in touch with their friends and family members while traveling. Others prefer not to get in touch and stay alone. Which do you prefer and why?

9. Some people prefer to go to the museum with their friends or colleagues, while others prefer to go alone. Which one do you prefer?

10. Do you agree or disagree with the following statement? Students can learn more if they have friends in class.

第八章　家　庭　关　系

一、核心话题真题

Some parents think they should prevent their children from making mistakes. Some think they should let them make mistakes. Which one do you think is better?

【话题解析】

家庭关系是一个比较抽象的话题,多考查父母和孩子之间的关系,尤其是父母对于孩子的家庭教育。首先我们要明确的是,children 这个英文单词的定义我们界定为 6~12 岁的孩子,并非青少年(teenager)。所以在这个话题中,对于这个年龄阶段孩子的学习能力、独立能力,考生的表达既不可以过低,也就是孩子完全不能管理自己,也不宜过高,如父母完全不应该干涉孩子。因此我们可以梳理出以下"万能"论点:

(1) 开阔视野。

offer a broad horizon/rich experience/correct mistakes

(2) 金钱支持。

families support individuals financially/provide monetary reward/ease financial burden

(3) 保护安全。

protect children/provide assistance/ensure safety/safety consciousness

(4) 心理疏导。

relieve or alleviate pressure/effective psychological counseling

二、核心词汇语料

misguided /ˌmɪsˈɡaɪdɪd/ *adj*. 被误导的

emotion /ɪˈmoʊʃn/ *n*. 情绪

fearful /ˈfɪrfl/ *adj*. 担心的；可怕的

chores /tʃɔːz/ *n*. 杂务；琐事

handle /ˈhændl/ *v*. 处理；对待

prepare /prɪˈper/ *v*. 准备

strive /straɪv/ *v*. 努力；奋斗

boost /buːst/ *v*. 提高；增加

deprive /dɪˈpraɪv/ *v*. 剥夺

independence /ˌɪndɪˈpendəns/ *n*. 独立

manage /ˈmænɪdʒ/ *v*. 管理

compromise /ˈkɑːmprəmaɪz/ *v*. 妥协

realize /ˈriəlaɪz/ *v*. 意识到

acknowledge /əkˈnɑːlɪdʒ/ *v*. 承认

intervene /ˌɪntərˈviːn/ *v*. 干涉

well-planned daily arrangement 计划好的每日安排

resilience and ingenuity 适应力与创造力

positive learning experience 积极的学习经历

contribute to 有助于

financial awareness 金钱意识

serious consequence 严重的后果

suffer from 遭受

psychologically beneficial　心理健康

deal with　处理

troubles and frustrations　困难与挫折

throw away　扔掉

三、满分回答 Sample

Some parents think they should prevent their children from making mistakes. Some think they should let them make mistakes. Which one do you think is better?

观点 Personally speaking，I think it's a good idea to allow students to make mistakes.

论点 1：Firstly，the ability to make mistakes can be a positive learning experience，psychologically beneficial. To be more specific，most of people don't realize they are wrong until they suffered from the serious consequence. The teenagers，who are in their period of striving to learn knowledge，can get much more experience when they make mistakes and then learn from it.

论点 2：On top of that，it is the responsibility of the parents to guide their children to the right path. That's to say，parents should give them right guidance since teenagers are easily misguided by others. Besides，some severe affairs，such as criminal case，can never be allowed because it can hardly be redeemed once it happens. So parents should educate their children to avoid such things.

四、变形题思路解析

1   It is important to maintain good relationship with family members than with friends. Do you agree or disagree? why?

选择 agree：

（1）同与朋友保持短期关系相比，与家庭成员相处更值得。

It's more worthwhile to keep a long-term relationship with our family, rather than a short-time one with friends.

（2）与家庭成员关系融洽能给我们提供经济帮助。

Keeping a good rapport with family can be financially beneficial.

观点   In my opinion, I agree with the statement.

论点 1：Firstly, it's more worthwhile to keep a long-term relationship with our family, rather than a short-time one with friends. That is to say, we spend countless time with our family members every day, a good relationship is necessary in day-to-day communications. However, there are some friends who we only meet in certain occasions that we would probably never see in each other's later lives, so trying to maintain something that's not long-standing is a waste of time and energy.

论点 2：On top of that, keeping a good rapport with family can be financially beneficial. For example, my mom would treat me a nice meal if I did the chores for her, and buy me the latest gadgets when I behave well in school，while friends wouldn't possibly be so generous to me that way.

2 Do you think it is a good idea for parents to give kids monetary reward if they have good grades in school? Please include details and examples in your explanation.

选择 agree：

(1) 这会激励孩子，让他们在学校表现好。

It would definitely motivate children to reinforce good school behavior.

(2) 这会让孩子有金钱意识。

This will cultivate children's financial awareness.

观点 From my perspective，I agree with the statement.

论点 1：Firstly，it would definitely motivate children to reinforce good school behavior. For example，if children can earn a shopping trip when they turn in all their homework for a week，they will form a habit of such behavior.

论点 2：In addition，this will cultivate children's financial awareness. To be more specific，children will realize money doesn't come for free，it has to be earned through real effort，they will be more careful next time they use it. It's a good chance for them to realize the role money plays in life.

3 Do you agree or disagree with the following statement? It is important to protect children from learning too soon about difficulties in life.

选择 disagree：

（1）在他们的成长过程中这是不可避免的。

It's inevitable in their growing process.

（2）幼年是一个很好的时机，家长可以教孩子调节压力和克服困难。

Early age can be an ideal time for adults to teach their children how to manage their life's stressors and get through challenges.

观点 From my perspective, I disagree with the statement.

论点 1：Firstly, it's inevitable in their growing process. To be more specific, difficulties are always there in every stage of life, even if they are young, how to get dressed and how to learn to read can always be problematic for them. Intervening in this can only delay their independence without contributing to the real problem, children have to face it someday and even learn that the hard way if we overprotect them.

论点 2：Apart from that, early age can be an ideal time for adults to teach their children how to manage their life's stressors and get through challenges. For example, my mom used to teach me how to deal with troubles and frustrations even since I was only five or six, it turned out to be very helpful in the later times and I can always throw the bad energy away when I was down for things.

4 Do you agree with the following statement? Parents should help their children solve problem.

选择 disagree：

（1）这会抑制孩子的适应力和创造力。

This will inhibit children's resilience and ingenuity.

（2）这会给家长增加大量的额外工作和压力。

This can add a huge amount of extra work and pressure to the parents.

观点 From my perspective, I disagree with the statement.

论点 1: Firstly, this will inhibit children's resilience and ingenuity. To be more specific, children are not born with the ability to solve problems and find solutions, they learn and develop this with practice, if parents intervene, the only way for children to develop the ability to solve problems will be deprived.

论点 2: On top of that, this can add a huge amount of extra work and pressure to the parents. For example, I had a classmate whose parents are always getting too involved with her homework, not only does she become too dependent on her parents, but her parents are also tired of being multi-taskers and do not have enough energy to deal with their own business.

5 It is not very good for a child to spend a short period of time living far away from home, visiting relatives and friends.

选择 agree：

（1）住在一个不熟悉的地方可能会有安全隐患。

Living in an unfamiliar place can sometimes bring unexpected safety hazard.

（2）这会给亲戚和朋友带来额外的麻烦。

This can cause additional trouble to their relatives and friends.

观点 From my perspective，I agree with the statement.

论点 1： Firstly，living in an unfamiliar place can sometimes bring unexpected safety hazard. For example，once I left home to visit a friend who lived in the countryside. To my surprise，the living condition there was very backward，especially the water quality. I still remember that I had at least three days of diarrhea after drinking the water.

论点 2： In addition，this can cause additional trouble to their relatives and friends. To be more specific，everyone has his fixed schedule for every day，so when the kid came over，the relatives or friends will need to spend extra effort to take care of the kid，not to mention elaborate dinners and well-planned daily arrangement，while they were also busy living their own life at the same time. So that's extra trouble a child brings should also be considered.

6 Some parents think they should prevent their children from making mistakes. Some think they should let them make mistakes. Which one do you think is better?

选择 let them make mistakes：

（1）培养孩子的社交能力、应对和适应能力是很重要的。

It's important for children to develop their social skills，coping and resilience skills.

（2）不犯错的孩子可能会缺乏自信，自我概念的培养也较欠缺。

Children that don't have opportunities to fail may have lower self-confidence and a less developed self-concept.

观点 From my perspective，I will go with the second one.

论点 1：Firstly，it's important for children to develop their social skills，coping and resilience skills. For example，if a child and a friend have an argument. Even though it is unpleasant，children learn to manage their emotions，take another's perspective，solve problems，and compromise. If parents swoop in to fix those problems，children miss out critical skill-building that results from learning from mistakes or failure.

论点 2：Furthermore，children that don't have opportunities to fail may have lower self-confidence and a less developed self-concept. That's to say，they tend to be more fearful of failure and less willing to try new things because they don't know how they will handle it.

7 　Do you agree or disagree that it is important for young people to learn some domestic skills like cooking，sewing and taking care of children?

选择 agree：

（1）生活会更简单。

Life will be easier.

（2）你可以在这个过程中学到很多。

You can learn a great deal during the process.

观点 　From my perspective，I agree with the statement.

论点 1：Firstly，life will be easier. Cooking a quick and easy meal for yourself can keep you full and healthy rather than going out to fill your stomach with some junk food，while sewing isn't difficult and it can help you perform maintenance on your clothing or other objects，which is also money-saving and eco-friendly.

论点 2: In addition，you can learn a great deal during the process. For example，every time I cook，I will search for various recipes online，and try to figure out the roles different seasoning play in one dish. So with the other chores，it turned out that my operational ability has greatly enhanced me every time I practiced.

8 Do you agree or disagree with the following statement? Children at an early age should learn independent living skills.

选择 agree：

(1) 及早学习生活技巧可以为孩子成年后解决难题做好准备。

Learning living skills early in life can prepare children to handle difficult problems in their adulthood.

(2) 孩子可能会在其中找到自己的兴趣。

Children might find their own passion on doing so.

 In my opinion，I totally agree with the statement.

论点 1: Firstly，learning living skills early in life can prepare children to handle difficult problems in their adulthood. For example，my mom taught me how to cook for myself when I was five，and this cooking skill really helped me a lot when I was locked down at home during coronavirus outbreak，since I had to cook for myself.

论点 2: Apart from this，children might find their own passion on doing so. If children are devoted to something like cooking，that takes up some time and boosts their creativity，they may be interested in cooking for others and pursue a chef career later in life，which is a way better than stick with video games or playing Barbie all day.

五、历年真题题库

1. Do you agree or disagree with the following sentence? With the increasing popularity of technology，parents should control children's access to social media.

2. Some people prevent their children from making mistakes or learn about difficulties in life，while others allow kids to do so. Which type of parents do you think is better?

3. Some people think parents should punish kids for their bad behaviors while others think parents should rewards kids for their good behaviors. Which do you think is better?

4. Do you agree or disagree with the following statement? It is important to allow children to use computers and other electronic devices as early in life as possible. Use reasons and details to explain your opinion.

第九章　成　功　要　素

一、核心话题真题

Do you agree or disagree that the determining factor of a student's success in school is the amount of intelligence?

【话题解析】

这类话题明显比之前几个话题更加抽象，因此很多同学在思考的时候会觉得比较困难，觉得自己想不到论点，或者想到论点了却无法找到合适的论据来论证，在表达过程中很容易掉入逻辑陷阱，那么接下来我们看看对于此类话题应该怎样回答。

成功要素类题目主要围绕着学习和工作，主要考查对于学习或工作来说，什么因素更重要，通常会有两个因素的对比，如天赋或努力哪个更重要，或者问某个因素是否是成功的决定性因素，如本章开头的例题："智商是否是学生成功的决定性因素？"

对于此类话题，我们总结出以下常用"万能"论点：

（1）时间效率。

do something in a timely manner/be more efficient

（2）人际社交。

communicative ability/soft skills in socialization/human resources

（3）实践技能。

hands on skills/practical ability/practice makes perfect

（4）个人品质。

independent/persistent/patient/competitive

二、核心词汇语料

communicative /kəˈmjuːnɪkeɪtɪv/　*adj*.交流的；健谈的

crucial /ˈkruːʃl/　*adj*.关键的

foundation /faʊnˈdeɪʃn/　*n*.基础

socialization /ˌsoʊʃələˈzeɪʃn/　*n*.社会化

talented /ˈtæləntɪd/　*adj*.有天赋的

permanent /ˈpɜːrmənənt/　*adj*.永久的

durable /ˈdʊrəbl/　*adj*.耐用的；持久的

negotiation /nɪˌɡoʊʃiˈeɪʃn/　*n*.谈判

consolidate /kənˈsɒlɪdeɪt/　*v*.巩固

competitive /kəmˈpetətɪv/　*adj*.有竞争力的

persistence /pərˈsɪstəns/　*n*.坚持；毅力

sympathy /ˈsɪmpəθi/　*n*.同情心；共情能力

group discussion　小组讨论

properly cooperate with others　恰当地与他人合作

go smoothly　顺畅进行

break the records　破纪录

review the knowledge　复习知识

modify mistakes　纠正错误

step by step　一步一步

hard work　努力工作

stick to authority　墨守成规

break through　突破

reach to an agreement　达成协议

present the ideas　表达想法

give the feedback　给出反馈

三、满分回答 Sample

Do you agree or disagree that the determining factor of a student's success in school is the amount of intelligence?

 Personally，I completely disagree with this statement.

论点 1：Firstly，students' communication skill is also crucial in cooperation. For instance，when I am in a group discussion，to achieve better results，I need to know how to properly cooperate with others，like listening to their opinions，sharing information and negotiating，etc. Such soft skills in socialization helps me to make sure that our work goes smoothly.

论点 2：Furthermore，persistence is also pretty essential. Take myself as an example，when I am memorizing English words，I would repeat several times to consolidate，not to mention my rehearsal for pronunciation. No matter how intelligent I am，practice makes perfect！

四、变形题思路解析

1 To be successful in sport，which is more important? Talent or hard work?

选择 hard work：

（1）对于体育来说，熟能生巧。

Practice makes perfect in sports.

（2）天赋并不是永恒的/长久的。

Talent is not permanent/durable.

观点 As for me，hard work is more important.

论点 1：To begin with，practice makes perfect in sports. Take myself as an example，when I tried skiing for the first time，I quickly fell down and lost my balance. But after one-month training with my coach，I gradually got used to master the gestures，board and ski poles. Right now，skiing becomes my favorite sports and I nail it through my practice！

论点 2：Secondly，talent is not durable. For instance，when I am preparing the running match in my school，my coach hopes me to beat all the professional athletes and break the records. So no matter how fast I am talented before，I have to start from new and challenge myself！

2 Do you agree or disagree that experienced teachers is a deciding factor to the success of a school?

选择 disagree：

(1) 老师也需要耐心。

Teachers also need to be patient.

(2) 校园设施建设对于一个学校的成功也很重要。

The campus equipment is also important for the success of a school.

观点 From my perspective，I disagree with this statement.

论点 1：Firstly，teachers also need to be patient. For instance，I had a new instructor one semester，she answered our questions so patiently：to review the knowledge，and to modify every mistakes step by step. Although it was her first-year teaching，we learned a lot.

论点 2：Moreover，the campus equipment is also important for the success of a school. Let's say，I study in an international bilingual school in Shanghai. It offers me all kinds of facilities like the library，scientific labs，gym and dining hall. These facilities allow me to study in a comfortable environment to back me up.

3 Do you agree or disagree that schools who encourage the development of students' creativity and imagination are likely to have more successful students? Use specific examples and details to explain your idea.

选择 agree：

（1）创造力使学生可以独立思考。

Creativity can enable students to develop their mind independently.

（2）想象力培养学生在社交中的共情能力。

Imagination also promotes students' social sympathy.

观点　As for me, I agree with this statement.

论点 1：First of all, creativity can enable students to develop their mind independently. For example, in a scientific experiment, if teachers encourage learners to come up with their own design and methods, they are more likely to explore new findings without sticking to authority.

论点 2：Secondly, imagination also promotes students' social sympathy. More specifically, in a group discussion, imaginative learners could better situate and imagine themselves in others' shoes. They are more capable to be empathetic and understand others' thoughts and feelings.

4　Do you agree or disagree with the following statement? Luck is as important as hard work for a person's success in the career.

选择 disagree：

（1）努力才是基础。

Hard work is the foundation.

（2）幸运并不是永恒的/长久的。

Luck is not permanent/durable.

观点 Personally speaking, I disagree with this statement.

论点 1: First of all, hard work is the foundation. Take my father as an example, as a businessman, successful business for him needs long-time preparation in advance like careful planning, research and investment. His company gradually grows bigger as his familiarity for the market and customers.

论点 2: In addition, luck is not durable. Let's say, in an interview, if my interviewer happens to prefer me just by luck without ability, I could not keep such luck for my future work. As long as I make some serious mistakes, the luck would disappear as I would be criticized.

5 Do you agree or disagree with the following statement? To be successful in life we should make enemies.

选择 agree：
(1) 有对手可以使人更有竞争力。
Enemies make people more competitive.
(2) 有对手可以提升我们做事的效率。
Enemies could enhance our efficiency of doing things.

观点 To be honest, I agree with this statement.

论点 1: First of all, enemies make people more competitive. Take myself as an example, in a debating match in my school, to win it, I trained myself to rehearse several times, like logically presenting the ideas and quickly giving the feedback. The existence of my enemies helps me challenge myself to break through.

论点 2：Secondly, enemies could enhance our efficiency. For example, when I am writing an essay with my classmates in the library. If I see their speed is faster or they are more focused, I don't dare to swipe my cellphone or watch short clips. I could get motivated to finish my task in a speedy manner.

6 Do you agree or disagree with the following statement? If you want to be successful in running a business, you need to maintain good relationship with others.

选择 agree：

(1) 我能为商业贸易积累人脉。

I could accumulate human resources for business trade.

(2) 我能使商业合作更顺畅。

I could make business cooperation more smoothly.

 As for me, I agree with this statement.

论点 1：To begin with, I could accumulate human resources for business trade. For instance, my father is a businessman who always attend business dinner or events. He told me it is a good chance for him to know more people and open more possibilities, like new investors or potential customers for the company's products.

论点 2：Furthermore, I could make business cooperation more smoothly. For example, in a business deal, if the manager always treats the partners with respects, like carefully listening to their needs and patiently discussing the project. The negotiation would be

easier to reach a consensus.

五、历年真题题库

1. Some people believe that it is the innate talents make a person an artist，while others think that it is the efforts a person put in that make the person an artist. Which do you prefer and why?

2. Do you agree or disagree with following statement? If you want to succeed in business，being outgoing and friendly is very important.

第十章　购物旅游消费

一、核心话题真题

Some people like to shop in large department stores or supermarkets to buy all things they need. Other people prefer to shop in small specialty stores or shops to buy one specific item at a time. Which do you prefer? Explain why.

【话题解析】

这个话题整体来说并不难,因为它还是比较贴近生活的。我们平时一定会买东西,不论是便利店还是超市。除此之外,这个题材的语料还可以和其他题材结合起来,回答各种各样的题目。

那么,我们再来具体地看一看这道题。这道题考查的是大超市和小商店的对比。其他的旅游购物花钱类题目,还会包含以下话题:是否要立刻买新出的电子产品,是否要保留旧的物件,旅游的时候玩一个地方还是玩几个地方等。对于这样的话题,无论我们选择的是哪个场景,我们都会发现,选择的目标都是为了省时间、省钱,因此我们对于这个题材可以梳理出以下"万能"论点:

(1) 节约很多时间。

save a lot of time

(2) 节省金钱。

not cost as much

（3）交通便利。

convenient transportation

（4）更好的服务。

better service

二、核心词汇语料

affordable /əˈfɔːrdəbl/　*adj*.负担得起的

update /ˌʌpˈdeɪt/　*n*.(软硬件)更新

costly /ˈkɔːstli/　*adj*.昂贵的

replacement /rɪˈpleɪsmənt/　*n*.替代品

show /ʃəʊ/　*n*.演出

play /pleɪ/　*n*.演出

energy /ˈenərdʒi/　*n*.能量;活力

landmark /ˈlændmɑːrk/　*n*.地标

spectacular /spekˈtækjələr/　*adj*.壮丽的

uniqueness /juːˈniːknɪs/　*n*.独特性

reasonable price　合理的价格

not that much to pay　不是特别贵

school break　假期

pursue a higher standard of sth.　追求更高级别的某物

right downstairs　就在楼下

grab some food　吃点东西

be struggling doing sth.　费很大力气做某事

full house　满场演出

spend wisely 明智地花钱

great deal 不错的买卖

best-selling 热销的

on sale 打折的

keep company with sb. 陪伴某人

accompany sb. 陪伴某人

local people 当地人

national park 国家公园

三、满分回答 Sample

Some people like to shop in large department stores or supermarkets to buy all things they need. Other people prefer to shop in small specialty stores or shops to buy one specific item at a time. Which do you prefer? Explain why.

观点 Personally speaking, I prefer to shop in small stores.

论点 1: Because well, first of all, I think it saves me a lot of time. There is a convenient store right downstairs where I live. Whenever I need anything, like toothpaste or some snacks, I would just go there and grab what I need. So it doesn't take more than a couple minutes and I can quickly go back to what I was working on.

论点 2: Besides, since I don't have a car, it would be hard for me to carry groceries all the way back. I remember a couple of years ago, I went to a Walmart on my own and got a lot of stuff. It was such a struggle to carry everything back home while I was

walking from the bus stop to home.

四、变形题思路解析

1 Some people think wearing fashionable clothing is important，while others not. Which do you agree?

选择 fashionable cloth is not important：

(1) 它花费很多时间。

It takes a lot of time.

(2) 时髦的衣服通常更贵。

Stylish clothes usually cost more.

观点 Personally speaking，I don't think wearing fashionable clothing is important.

论点 1：First of all，it takes too much time. If we are to keep up with the trends，we will be shopping often because fashionable things go out of date quickly. So we might need to go to the mall every now and then. We could totally use this time to do something else like hanging out with friends.

论点 2：Second of all，stylish clothes usually cost more. Take my mom as an example，she buys a lot of those fancy dresses and coats，which can be a couple of thousands dollars. I just don't feel like they are worth the price.

2 Which one do you prefer? To buy the newly-released e-product as soon as possible or to wait for a while and buy it.

选择 wait for a while：

(1) 电子产品的价格可能会在一段时间后下降。

The price of e-products are likely to decrease after a while.

(2) 新产品带来的一些问题将随着更新得到修复。

Some bugs that come with the new products will be fixed with the updates.

观点 Personally speaking，I would like to wait for a while.

论点 1： First of all，the price of e-products is likely to decrease after a while. I remember when I was trying to get an iPhone 13，it was pretty expensive first released，more than seven thousand yuan. But after a couple of months，when I looked it up again in one of those shopping Apps，it got a discount of ten percent which was definitely a great deal for me.

论点 2： Second of all，there might be some bugs or defects that come with the new products. Take my mom as an example，she purchased the brand new iPad on the first day of release. But she soon found out that the Apple pencil was having connection problems.

3 Some people like to keep old objects with them while others throw old stuff away. Which do you prefer? Why?

选择 keep old objects：

(1) 旧的东西可能还有用。

Old stuff might still be useful.

（2）如果我们以后要用的话还得买新的，很贵。

If we want them in the future, we will have to buy replacements and that costs a lot of money.

观点 Personally speaking, I would like to keep old objects.

论点 1：First of all, old stuff might be useful one day. Take my old chair as an example, I already got two chairs in my room so I was actually considering throwing them away. But when we renovated our dining room, I found that it fits perfectly into our new furniture.

论点 2：Second of all, it would cost a lot if we happen to need them in the future. For instance, when I was moving to a new apartment last month, I had to buy a new mattress because I threw the old one last year. I wasn't really expecting this, and it was such a pity.

五、历年真题题库

1. Some people prefer to travel to some new places that they have never been, while others prefer to travel to places that they have been before. Which do you prefer? Why?

2. Do you agree or disagree with the following statement? Traveling to new places would be a pleasant memory instead of a time-consuming and energy-burning task.

3. Some people prefer to spend lots of money on vacation, some people spend little money on vacation. Which do you prefer?

4. When traveling outside, some people prefer to keep connections with their family members and friends, while other people do not prefer to do so. Which way do you prefer? Why?

5. When visiting museums, simply admiring the works or taking photographs, which do you prefer?

6. Do you agree with the following statement? When visiting a country for the first time, it is important to know their tradition and culture.

7. Some people prefer to go to the museum with their friends or colleagues, while others prefer to go alone. Which one do you prefer?

8. Some people think that risk-taking activities such as rock-climbing and skydiving require a lot of bravery, while others think this is not brave, but simply foolish. Which view do you agree with? Explain why.

9. If you are going to travel to a new country for a week, do you prefer to travel to a major city in the country or to several different places?

10. Some people like to make plans in advance when they decide to travel, while others prefer to make decisions when they are traveling. Which do you prefer?

11. Imagine that you and your friends are going to hang out, and you guys need to decide where to go. Who do you think should make the decision? You make it, or you and your friends make it together. Why? Use specific reasons and examples to explain

your choice.

12. When it comes to buying daily necessities, some people prefer to shop in grocery stores now and then to gather all the things they need, while others prefer to go to a supermarket and buy everything all at once. Which do you prefer? Why?

13. Some people prefer to buy a product as soon as it is in the market, while other people prefer to purchase a product when it has been in the market for some time. Which do you prefer? Why?

第十一章　媒体科技

一、核心话题真题

Which of the following can be better sources of news? Newspapers or TV.

【话题解析】

媒体与科技类话题近来常常考到，一般与网络报纸、电视节目等相关。比如以上例题："你认为电视和报纸哪个是更好的新闻渠道？"这类话题与我们生活的相关性比较大，大家平时对于这些话题的想法也比较多，但是许多同学在回答此类问题的时候却不能保持良好的输出逻辑。因此我们不能掉以轻心，还是需要多多练习，梳理清楚话题表达的结构。

对于这类话题，我们为大家总结整理了以下常用"万能"论点：

（1）时间效率。

time-efficient/save more time

（2）趣味放松。

release my pressure/more entertaining

（3）与时俱进。

more up-to-date/keep up to changes

（4）获得知识。

acquire various knowledge/more informative

(5) 人际社交。

bond with sb./avoid embarrassment/more sincere

(6) 培养兴趣。

develop interests

二、核心词汇语料

informative /ɪnˈfɔːmətɪv/   *adj.* 提供信息的

witness /ˈwɪtnəs/   *v.* 目击；*n.* 目击者

imitate /ˈɪmɪteɪt/   *v.* 模仿

reflect /rɪˈflekt/   *v.* 反应

ignore /ɪɡˈnɔːr/   *v.* 忽略

scandal /ˈskændl/   *n.* 丑闻

soap opera   肥皂剧

up-to-date   最新的

entertainment program   娱乐节目

take a break   休息

hilarious plot   滑稽的情节

global affair   全球事务

sincere attitude   真诚的态度

political decision   政治决策

economical trend   经济趋势

ecological crisis   生态危机

big fan   狂热的粉丝

biased view   偏见

broaden someone's horizon   开阔眼界

bond with   和……一起

三、满分回答 Sample

Which of the following can be better sources of news? Newspapers or TV.

 观点   As for me，I think TV is a better source of news.

论点 1：Firstly，television is more informative than newspapers. For example，I am a big fan of TV since it contains different channels as entertainment，international news and education. I could easily find the suitable one to have fun or learn something new.

论点 2：Additionally，television is more up-to-date. To be more specific，TV offers me 24-hour cable news network of live streaming. I could witness what happened more directly and immediately，rather than waiting for the publication of newspapers.

四、变形题思路解析

1   Some people prefer to watch entertainment programs on TV. Others prefer to watch educational programs. Which do you prefer? Explain why.

选择 entertaining programs：

(1) 我能更好地缓解压力。

I could better release my pressure.

(2) 我能更大程度地和家人一起享受家庭时光。

I could bond with family to a larger extent.

观点 From my perspective, I prefer to watch entertainment programs.

论点 1: To begin with, it could better release my pressure. Take myself as an example, during my hectic study or work schedule, I could relax myself by laughing at the jokes in the talk show or comedies in entertaining channels. As a result, my mind would be eased by taking a break.

论点 2: Secondly, I could bond with family to a larger extent. Let's say, after my family dinner, Chinese sitcom or soap operas are our favorite choice when hanging out together. It is so enjoyable for us to discuss the hilarious plots, and imitate the comedians' actions.

2 Which kind of movies do you prefer? Movies that are exciting and entertaining or more serious ones with important message.

选择 serious movies:

(1) 严肃的电影可以让我们获得各种各样的知识。

Serious movies can make us acquire various knowledge.

(2) 它能培养更多兴趣。

It can develop/explore more interest.

观点 Personally，I prefer to choose serious movies with important message.

论点 1：To start up，it functions to acquire various knowledge. For example，I could easily access different subjects as physics，chemistry or geography to choose corresponding documentaries. I would like to watch biography of important celebrities like Steve Jobs，I could definitely learn from his persistence.

论点 2：And also，I could develop my interests. Let's say，previously，I knew nothing about hip-hop. After I watched a movie of *8 Miles*，it reflects how Eminem composes hip-hop lyrics and rhymes. I gradually fall in love with this form of art and even create my own flows.

3 Some people think it's better to read or watch negative news than positive news. Do you agree or disagree with this idea?

选择 agree：

(1) 负面新闻可以帮助我们警醒/反思自身。

Negative news help us alarm/reflect ourselves.

(2) 我们可以想办法为社会贡献自己的力量。

We can find ways to contribute our efforts for society.

观点 As for me，I agree with this statement.

论点 1：Firstly，audience could easily alarm themselves through negative news. For instance，when some celebrities' scandals are exposed like drugs，traffic speeding，or tax evasion，people would be shocked and even associate themselves to avoid such illegal

behaviors.

论点 2：In addition，people could find ways to contribute their efforts for society. Take my parents as an example，when they see some news of disaster like flood，tornado or earthquake，they would feel empathetic and make some donation like money or clothes for people in need.

4 Do you agree or disagree with the following statement? People should spend time watching news from other countries.

选择 agree：

（1）这让我们与时俱进。

It can make us keep up-to-date.

（2）这让我们学习外语。

It can make us learn foreign language.

观点 From my perspective，I totally agree with this statement.

论点 1：To begin with，it works to keep me up-to-date. For example，by watching international news on TV，I get to know more about global affairs like political decisions，economic trends or ecological crisis. Such various news makes me more informative.

论点 2：Moreover，it is beneficial for me to learn foreign language. For instance, I am a big fan of watching social news of FOX channel in the US，it could broaden my horizon when I listen to the reporters' professional pronunciation，learn some slang and

even promote my language sense for English.

5 Do you agree with the statement that the best way to know a country is to watch its TV program?

选择 disagree：

（1）电视节目往往以狭隘的观点来展示一个国家最好的一面。

TV programs tend to show the best of a country as biased views.

（2）外国电视节目有语言障碍。

Foreign TV programs have language barrier.

观点 Personally speaking, I disagree with this statement.

论点 1：First of all, TV programs tend to show the best of a country as biased views. To be more specific, the travelling channel would only shoot the beautiful scenes in the country. The negative sides of poverty or disaster are rarely shown. So audience could not get a full picture of the country.

论点 2：Besides, foreign TV programs have language barrier. Take myself as an example, when I was a newbie in English study, I felt so confused and even stressed to watch international news. The pronunciation, words and grammar sound too unfamiliar for me to make sense.

6 People in the past liked board games and card games, while now people like playing video games on their computers and smartphones. Which do you prefer?

选择 video games：

（1）一种与朋友联系的更流行的方式。

It is a more popular way to bond with my friends.

（2）这更节约时间/方便。

It is more time-efficient/convenient.

观点 As for me, I prefer to play video games.

论点 1：Firstly, it is a more popular way to bond with my friends. Take myself as an example, almost ninety percent of my classmates download the mobile game of *Angry Birds*. After school work, we are eager to have some rounds and compare our scores. It is definitely a common topic and interest to share with.

论点 2：Plus, it is more convenient. For instance, I would like to play several cellphone games during class break or traffic time by car. It's usually needs ten minutes per round without carrying any materials like the chess board or paper cards. It more portable to bring my laptop or smartphone.

7 When receiving message of friends, some people prefer to reply it right way, others however prefer to reply it after a while. Which method do you prefer? Explain why.

选择 reply it right way：

（1）这可以节约时间。

It's more time-efficient.

（2）这能避免更深的误解。

It can avoid further misunderstanding.

观点 Personally，I prefer to reply it right way.

论点 1：First of all，it could be more time-efficient. Let's say，if I am discussing an important issue of groupwork with my friends，I need our mutual response in time to move forward. Otherwise，the whole project would be delayed and might miss the deadline.

论点 2：Besides，I could better avoid further misunderstanding. Take myself as an example，if I just had a fight with my best friend Jenny，I would be super sensitive for her messages. If she doesn't respond me immediately，I would think she ignores me and even break our friendship.

8 Do you agree or disagree with the following statement? Talking face-to-face in person is a better way to communicate than communicating through emails and by text messages.

选择 disagree：
（1）邮件和短信更方便。
Emails and text messages are more convenient.
（2）这可以避免尴尬。
It works to prevent embarrassment.

观点 Personally speaking，I disagree with this statement.

论点 1: To start up, emails and text messages are more convenient. Take myself as an example, if I want to chat with people from a new club, I don't have to schedule our meetings and find an available time for both of us. I could just leave my phone number and text them at any time during the day.

论点 2: In addition, it works to prevent embarrassment. For instance, I tend to be shy when I firstly get to know some new friends in a party. In this case, texting gives me more space to think about my language, find the interesting topics, and ease my fear.

9 Do you agree or disagree with the following statement? It's impolite to make calls or send text messages on a diner table. Please explain in details.

选择 agree：

(1) 这会导致尴尬。

It would cause embarrassment.

(2) 这也会耽误时间。

It would also be time-consuming.

 From my perspective, I agree with this statement.

论点 1: First, it would cause embarrassment. Let's say, in a social event of business dinner, people there barely know each other, so a sudden call would shock everyone and disrupt their conversations. In this case, I don't feel comfortable also as I would be stared by all the strangers.

论点 2: Secondly, it would also be time-consuming. For example, if I am updating

my recent school life with parents in a family dinner, the calls or texts would distract my focus and I have to stop my sharing. And my parents also have to wait for me to finish the calls, which would make them think I am not respectful and ignore their feelings.

10 Some trains now provide quiet compartments where people aren't allowed to talk loudly or use cellphones, laptops. Some people tend to disagree. What do you think?

选择 agree：

(1) 它能创造一个更舒适的环境。

It can shape a more comfortable place.

(2) 我们能更好地欣赏旅途景色。

We can better appreciate the sceneries alongside.

观点 Personally speaking, I agree with such quite compartments.

论点 1：Firstly, it could shape a more comfortable place. For example, my little sister Amy used to sleep in train, so any loud conversation or sounds of electronic devices would wake her up immediately. Such quite compartments benefit her from having a rest during traveling or commuting.

论点 2：Secondly, it is better to appreciate the sceneries alongside. Take myself as an example, once I took a train to go home alone, and my electronic devices ran out of power. Then I happened to notice the sky, grassland, and mountains outside the window without any distraction.

11 Which one do you prefer when you have a disagreement with your friends? Speaking directly face to face and through phone calls or sending an email and a text message.

选择 speaking face to face：

（1）我能体现真诚的态度。

I can show my sincere attitude.

（2）发短信可能会导致更深的误解。

Texting might lead to deeper misunderstanding.

观点 From my perspective，I prefer to speak face to face with my friends.

论点 1：To begin with，I could show my sincere attitude. For example，if I argue with my best friend Jenny and even have a fight，I would talk to her in person to let her really feel my sincerity. I could use my body language to give her a hug or make some funny smile for her to ease her anger.

论点 2：On top of that，texting might lead to deeper misunderstanding. For instance，after the disagreement，if I see my apologizing messages left unread，I would think my friends deliberately ignore me and don't respect me at all. As a result，our friendship would be broken.

五、历年真题题库

1. Do you agree or disagree with the following statement? It's impolite to make calls

or send text messages on a diner table. Explain in details.

2. Some trains now provide quiet compartments where people aren't allowed to talk loudly or use cellphones，laptops. Some people tend to disagree. What do you think?

3. Which one do you prefer when you have a disagreement with your friends? Speaking directly face to face and through phone calls or sending an email and a text message.

第十二章 政府社会

一、核心话题真题

The school is going to open the library to the general public and charge some fee if citizens need to borrow some books. Do you think it's a good idea or not?

【话题解析】

这个话题可能是同学们不太熟悉的一个话题。很多同学可能在日常生活中并没有思考过这类问题。即便思考过，也可能是从一个比较宏观的角度去看的。但是在托福口语考试里，切忌从太过理论化、太过深奥的角度去阐述答案，因为我们在考试中答题时间只有45秒。同学们需要更多地从直观的角度回答问题。

那么，我们再来具体地看一看这道题。这道题考查的是"如果学校图书馆向大众开放借书，要不要收费"的问题。其他政府、社会类话题，除了包含收费问题，还会有建造某些设施、给大众提供免费课程、普通人参与竞选等问题。对于这类话题，我们的回答可以包含以下几个方面：会不会给市民提供便利、会不会影响其他人、是否会污染环境、是否会太有压力等，因此我们可以梳理出以下"万能"论点：

(1) 给市民提供便利。

provide some convenience to citizens

(2) 影响在校学生的学习。

influence the learning of students in school

（3）污染环境。

pollute the environment

（4）给人造成过多压力。

create too much stress for people

（5）改善基础设施。

improve the infrastructure

二、核心词汇语料

retirement /rɪˈtaɪərmənt/　*n*. 退休

infrastructure /ˈɪnfrəstrʌktʃər/　*n*. 基础设施

implement /ˈɪmplɪment/　*v*. 实施

expenditure /ɪkˈspendɪtʃər/　*n*. 支出

authority /əˈθɔːrəti/　*n*. 当局

consequence /ˈkɑːnsɪkwens/　*n*. 后果

officially /əˈfɪʃəli/　*adv*. 正式地

community /kəˈmjuːnəti/　*n*. 社区,社群

fund /fʌnd/　*n*. 资金

current students　录取的学生

enrolled students　在读学生

sports field　运动场

do sth. with caution　小心地做某事

greenhouse effect　温室效应

financial support　财政资助

allocate budget　分配预算

be of top priority　最重要的

chain effect　连锁反应

preferential policies　优惠政策

social welfare　社会福利

increase public awareness of sth.　增强公众对某事的意识

in an effort to do sth.　为了达到某个目的

long-term effects　长期影响

short-term effects　短期影响

strengthen the relationship between　加强……之间的关系

三、满分回答 Sample

The school is going to open the library to the general public and charge some fee if citizens need to borrow some books. Do you think it's a good idea or not?

观点 Personally speaking, I do think the school should charge some fee.

论点 1：First of all, I think lending books to the general public would create problems that need money to fix. For example, citizens might not handle the book with caution. They could accidentally damage the pages, spill food or drinks onto the books or even make some notes which can be uncomfortable for the next reader. We will need the money to replace those damaged books.

论点 2：Besides, it would help to improve the educational infrastructure at school. We could use the money to upgrade the projector, sports fields, or to purchase some extra public computers for students who can't afford one.

四、变形题思路解析

1 Do you agree or disagree the following statement? People should retire after sixty-five.

选择 disagree：

（1）他们需要更多的时间陪伴家人和享受生活。

They need more time to keep accompany with their family and enjoy life.

（2）他们的工作效率降低。

They don't work as efficient any more.

观点 Personally speaking，I do not think people should retire after sixty-five.

论点 1：First of all，these people need more time to keep accompany with their family. Take my uncle as an example，he retired last year and stayed at home. He used to be so busy that most of the time when he got back from work at late nights，his family would have already fallen asleep.

论点 2：Second of all，they don't work as efficient. I remember my grandpa was working as an accountant at an advanced age. But he soon started forgetting things and making all the mistakes.

2 Your community has been donated a piece of land, should it be used to build an amusement center or grow plant and flowers?

选择 grow plant and flower：

(1) 这会改善空气质量。

It helps to improve the air quality.

(2) 这会给市民提供休息的场地。

It provides the citizens with a place to relax.

观点 Personally speaking, I think we should grow plants and flower.

论点 1：First of all, plants and flowers help to improve the air quality through the process of photosynthesis. Plants absorb carbon dioxide and produce oxygen. In this way, they offset greenhouse effect in some way for the city.

论点 2：Second of all, that is going to be a place for people to relax. No one would hate to breath some fresh air in the middle of a crowed city. Take myself as an example, I would take a ten-minute walk every day in a green area next to my neighborhood, which is really refreshing.

3 Do you agree or disagree with building a factory that provides many jobs but pollutes the environment?

选择 disagree：

(1) 环境变差危害市民的身体健康。

A polluted environment harms the physical health of citizens.

（2）以环境为代价的工厂很难长久。

Factories that develop at the expense of environment will not be sustainable.

观点 Personally speaking, I don't think it's a good idea to build such a factory.

论点 1: First of all, a polluted environment harms the health of citizens. I remember a couple years ago when there was a serious smog in Beijing, the pollution caused serious health problems for millions of people living there, especially the newborns and kids. It took the government a long time to get rid of the pollution.

论点 2: Second of all, factories that develop at the expense of environment will not be sustainable. In the same example of Beijing, the factories with excessive emission were all shut down by the government soon after the problems were reported.

4 Your university decided to allow local citizens to listen in the campus. They could enter the class, but can't ask questions and don't have assignments. Do you agree or not agree?

选择 disagree：

（1）他们会影响课堂的质量。

They will affect the quality of the class.

（2）教授会有一些额外的工作。

Professors will have some extra work to do.

观点 Personally speaking, I don't think it's a great idea to allow locals to listen.

论点1：First of all, they will affect the quality of class. Since they don't have to do all the reading and assignments ahead of time, they will be asking some basic questions. This is going to slow down the class discussion for those who are taking the class for credits.

论点2：Second of all, professors will have some extra work to do even if they don't have assignments. For example, professor will have to remember extra names or prepare extra handouts. These little things add up and require professors' attention.

五、历年真题题库

1. Some people think historical sites should be open to the general public, but some people think historical sites should only be open to experts and researchers. Which do you think is better?

2. Do you think it's a good idea to elect people from ordinary background to be government leaders?

3. Your community has received money from the government to build a building in an open area. Which would you prefer, a company offering more jobs or a park? Use specific examples and details to support your answer.

4. Your community wants to help elder people feel more comfortable with computers. Which one do you think better? Giving lectures to all elder people together or recruiting students to tutor the elderly individually.

第二部分

综合任务

Task 2 ~ Task 4

第十三章　Task 2

一、Increase Workspace at the Computer Lab

I think the university should increase the amount of desktop workspace around each computer in the computer lab. Currently, the computers are tightly packed together, so there is not enough room to spread out all your papers and books to look at them, which makes working on written assignments and research papers difficult. More space could be created by removing some computers. Since the lab is not very crowded with students, there are always several unused computers when I go there, so removing some computers should not be a problem.

Sincerely,

Jennifer Stanley

1. 词汇分析1

desktop /'desktɒp/　n. 台式电脑；桌面

workspace /'wɜːrkspeɪs/　n. 工作空间

packed /pækt/　adj. 塞满的, 压紧的

crowded /'kraʊdɪd/　adj. 拥挤的

written assignment 书面作业

research paper 研究论文

spread out 传播

2. 信息提取

The university should increase the amount of desktop workspace around each computer in the computer lab.

3. 听力原文

(male student) Did you see Jennifer's letter in the paper today?

(female student) Yeah why?

(male student) Oh well, it's just that I don't agree with her. I don't think they should do that.

(female student) Oh no. How come?

(male student) Well, I think she's exaggerating the problem. I mean, it may be true that you don't have room to arrange everything in front of you while you are doing an assignment, but there's more than enough space to look at, maybe two or three books at a time, which is plenty.

(female student) Yeah, that's probably enough room in most cases.

(male student) Right. With most assignments, you really only need to be able to see a few books or articles. I mean, how many things can you look at once?

(female student) Well, but if it wouldn't be a problem to do what she suggests, why not do it?

(male student) Yeah, but I think it would be a problem. I mean, she must not be going at night because I go at night and it's often pretty crowded sometimes you have to wait in line to use a computer.

(female student) Oh, really? I hadn't realized it gets so busy at night.

(male student) Yeah, she must be going during the day, when it's less crowded, when a lot of people are in class. But at night, it's much busier, so I don't think what she's suggesting would work.

4. 词汇分析 2

exaggerate /ɪɡˈzædʒəreɪt/　v. 夸张

arrange /əˈreɪndʒ/　v. 安排

suggest /səˈdʒest/　v. 建议

realize /ˈriəlaɪz/　v. 实现，意识到

busier /ˈbɪzɪər/　adj. 更忙碌

wait in line　排队等候

5. 范例答案

In the proposal, the student suggests the university increase the amount of desktop workspace around each computer in the computer lab.

First, there is not enough room to spread out papers and books.

Second, there are always several unused computers.

However, in the conversation, the man disagrees with this proposal.

First, he says that the student is exaggerating the problem. It may be true that students don't have room to arrange everything in front of them while doing an assignment, but there's more than enough space to look at, maybe two or three books at a time, which is plenty. With most assignments, they only need to be able to see a few books or articles.

Second, he mentions that it's often pretty crowded sometimes at night, and students have to wait in line to use a computer. During the day, it could be less crowded, when a lot of people are in class. But at night, it's much busier, so the proposal would not work.

二、Graduate Students Should Speak at Information Sessions

The university regularly hosts information sessions about graduate school for undergraduates who are interested in pursuing advanced degrees after graduation and want to learn more. These sessions are now led by university staff，but I think the university should start inviting graduate students to also speak to the undergraduates. I believe that hearing from graduate students would help undergraduates more fully understand what to expect in graduate school，since the graduate students could share their experiences. Since including graduate students would make the sessions longer，it might be helpful to have multiple sessions based on specific subject areas，and students could attend one that fits their academic interests.

Sincerely，

Ted Myers

1. 词汇分析 1

host /hoʊst/　*n*. 主人，大量；*v*. 款待，主办（宴会等），主持节目

undergraduate /ˌʌndərˈgrædʒuət/　*n*. 本科生

pursue /pərˈsuː/　*v*. 追求；追逐

advanced /ədˈvænst/　*adj*. 先进的，高级的，高等的；（发展）晚期的

invite /ˈɪnvaɪt/　*v*. 邀请

multiple /ˈmʌltɪpl/　*adj*. 数量多的，多种多样的；*n*. 倍数

fit /fɪt/　*adj*. 健康的，适合的；*v*. 适合，安置

information session　宣讲会

2. 信息提取

The university should start inviting graduate students to speak to the undergraduates at the information sessions.

3. 听力原文

(female student)Hmmm, this a really good idea.

(male student)Yeah, that would be cool.

(female student)Yeah, I think it could be helpful. I went to one of those last month and right now we pretty much just get information about stuff like academic requirements and the application process. Not much else.

(male student)And there's a lot more to it than that.

(female student)Yeah, and since they're living it. We hear more about the day-to-day experience and the reality of being there.

(male student)Yeah, I see how that would be helpful.

(female student)Right. Like my sister who's studying for a Ph. D. in history, she said something about how since her classes don't meet as often as undergraduate classes. It can be hard to stay motivated, cause there's so much unstructured time between classes.

(male student)Yeah, it would be good to hear about things like that. So it's not a surprise.

(female student)Right, and even if it means they'll need to reorganize like she's saying. I think that could be good, since experiences won't be the same for all fields.

(male student)That's true.

(female student)I mean, doing a degree in history is different from doing one in chemistry. The content, the requirements and the types of jobs that graduates can go onto won't be the same for all programs. So, it would be helpful to keep the discussions more focused.

(male student)Sure，here about specific programs.

(female student)Right，that way students could get the most out of it.

4. 词汇分析2

reality /rɪˈæləti/　n. 真实情况

motivated /ˈmoʊtɪveɪtɪd/　adj. 积极的

reorganize /riˈɔːrɡəˈnaɪz/　v. 重组

content /ˈkɒntent/　n. 内容，容量，目录；v. 满足

program /ˈproɡræm/　n. 节目，计划；v. 编写程序，使……按计划进行

discussion /dɪˈskʌʃ(ə)n/　n. 讨论

focused /ˈfoʊkəst/　adj. 注意力集中的

application process　申请流程

day-to-day experience　日常经历

get the most out of it　充分利用

5. 范例答案

In the proposal，the student suggests that the university should start inviting graduate students to speak to the undergraduates at information sessions apart from staff.

First，it helps undergraduates more fully understand what to expect in graduate school.

Second，students could attend one of several that fits their academic interests.

In the conversation，the woman agrees with this proposal.

First，she says that she only got information like academic requirements and the application process from staff last month，nothing else. Graduate students living it so they can share more about the day-to-day experience，showing the reality of being there. Plus，her sister who's studying for a Ph. D. in history，found it hard to stay motivated since her classes don't meet as often as undergraduate classes, since there's so much unstructured time between classes.

Second, she mentions that experiences won't be the same for all fields if they are reorganized. Say, doing a degree in history is different from doing one in chemistry. For example, the content, requirements and the types of jobs that graduates can go onto won't be the same for all programs. So, it would be helpful to keep the discussions more focused.

三、No More Jazz Choir

Currently, the university has a jazz choir, a group of students who meet to sing jazz music and give concerts. However, starting next year the jazz choir will be discontinued, and will no longer exist. The primary reason for ending the jazz choir, according to the director, is that students' interest in participating has been low, and it has been difficult to find enough student singers to fill the jazz choir. He mentioned that there will still be an opportunity for students to participate in a singing group, since the university also has another choir that performs concerts on campus, so students can participate in the other choir instead.

1. 词汇分析 1

choir /ˈkwaɪər/ *n*. 唱诗班

concert /ˈkɒnsət/ *n*. 音乐会

discontinue /ˌdɪskənˈtɪnju/ *v*. 停止

exist /ɪgˈzɪst/ *v*. 存在

primary /ˈpraɪməri/ *adj*. 主要的

director /dəˈrektər/　　*n*. 理事,经理

participate /paːrˈtɪsɪpeɪt/　*v*. 参加

fill /fɪl/　*v*: 填满

perform /pərˈfɔːrm/　　*v*. 执行,表演

no longer　不再

2. 信息提取

Starting next year the jazz choir will be discontinued.

3. 听力原文

(male student) Alicia, did you see this article in today's paper? Aren't you involved with that group?

(female student) I am. And I think it's a shame they're doing this. I don't think they should.

(male student) Well, but I guess their reasoning makes sense. Maybe it's not worth it for the director.

(female student) I get that. But the real problem is that we have a really intense rehearsal schedule. We need to rehearse three days a week. And for a lot of students, that's just too much of a commitment.

(male student) Yeah, three meetings a week is a lot.

(female student) Right. On top of concerts, it is a lot. I think if they just reduced it and have rehearsals maybe once a week, then I bet lots of students could do it.

(male student) That makes sense. But even so, at least there's an alternative. Right?

(female student) Yeah, but it's not the same.

(male student) Oh no! Why?

(female student) Because the music they do is totally different. All they do is

classical music. And personally, I don't like that music as much.

(male student) Hmm ... Yeah. That makes a difference. I suppose a lot of students feel that way.

(female student) Definitely.

4. 词汇分析2

involved /ɪnˈvɒlvd/ *adj.* 参与，作为一部分，有关联

shame /ʃeɪm/ *adj.* 羞愧的；*v.* 使羞愧

intense /ɪnˈtens/ *adj.* 强烈的，激烈的

rehearse /rɪˈhɜːrs/ *v.* 排练

rehearsal /rɪˈhɜːrsl/ *n.* 排练

schedule /ˈskedʒuːl/ *v.* 安排，预定；*n.* 日程安排，明细表，工作计划

commitment /kəˈmɪtmənt/ *n.* 承诺，投入，保证，许诺

alternative /ɔːlˈtɜːrnətɪv/ *adj.* 可供替代的，非传统的；*n.* 可供选择的事物

suppose /səˈpoʊz/ *v.* 假设

make sense 有道理，讲得通

5. 范例答案

In the announcement, the university announces that the jazz choir will be discontinued next year.

First, students' interest in participating has been low, and it has been difficult to find enough student singers to fill the jazz choir.

Second, the university also has another choir for students to participate in.

However, in the conversation, the woman disagrees with this announcement.

First, she says that the real problem is that they have a really intense rehearsal schedule to rehearse three days a week. And for a lot of students, that's just too much commitment on the concerts. Therefore, she believes that lots of students could do it if the university can reduce the time of rehearsals to once a week.

Second，she mentions that the alternative plan is not the same，because the music is totally different. All they do is classical music. And she doesn't like that music as much.

四、No Credit for Outside Classes

Greenwood University (GU) students who return home to other parts of the country over the summer sometimes take classes at other universities with the goal of receiving enough additional credits to graduate early. However，beginning next year，the university will no longer give credit for any courses taken at other institutions. The administration is concerned that not all universities meet our own rigorous academic standards. GU has decided，however，to lower tuition on its own summer courses to make it affordable for out-of-town students to take classes here during the summer and still have the opportunity to graduate early if they wish.

1. 词汇分析 1

return /rɪˈtɜːrn/　*n*. 返回,恢复;*v*. 返回,回报

goal /goʊl/　*n*. 目标

receive /rɪˈsiːv/　*v*. 接收

institution /ˌɪnstɪˈtuːʃn/　*n*. 制度,建立

administration /ədˌmɪnɪˈstreɪʃn/　*n*. 行政,执行

rigorous /ˈrɪɡərəs/　*adj*. 谨慎的,细致的,彻底的,严格的

standard /ˈstændərd/　*n*. 标准;*adj*. 通常的

tuition /tuˈɪʃn/　*n*. 学费

affordable /əˈfɔːrdəbl/　*adj*. 负担得起的

additional credit   额外的学分

2. 信息提取

Beginning next year，the university will no longer give credit for any courses taken at other institutions.

3. 听力原文

(female student) Wow，I think this is way too extreme. Quite a few students rely on this.

(male student) Yeah，I know. But I took a chemistry class near home last summer and it seemed a little easier than science classes here.

(female student) Well，maybe. I get that they're concerned. Not every class at every school is the same. But they could handle it on a case by case basis.

(male student) What do you mean? How?

(female student) Why not just make students submit a request ahead of time? Students could find course and then send in the course outline for the class they want to take.

(male student) Yeah，those are pretty easy to find online. Or you could always ask the professor.

(female student) Right. So show that to the office here at GU and then they can decide if it's good enough. Like they could have told you that the chemistry course didn't cover the same things and not accept it. That's fair. But that wouldn't always be the case.

(male student) OK. I see. Yeah. But you can always stay here over the summer. It sounds like they're making it easier to do that.

(female student) I don't think what they're doing will help as much as they think. I still have to get housing and that's a big expense. The reason students go to stay at home and study near there is to save money.

(male student) Yeah，it's still free to live at home. You can't beat that.

(female student) Exactly. Plus，you want to spend time with your family and your friends back home，especially after we've been away so long.

4．词汇分析2

extreme /ɪkˈstriːm/　*adj*．极端的；*n*．极度，极端的情况

handle /ˈhændl/　*v*．处理；*n*．把手

submit /səbˈmɪt/　*v*．提交，顺从

request /rɪˈkwest/　*n*．要求；*v*．要求

outline /ˈaʊtlaɪn/　*v*．概述；*n*．概述

chemistry /ˈkemɪstri/　*n*．化学

expense /ɪkˈspens/　*n*．费用，开支

on a case by case basis　按特殊情况处理

ahead of time　提前

5．范例答案

In the announcement，the university announces that it will no longer give credit for any courses taken at other institutions next year.

First，not all universities meet the university's own rigorous academic standards.

Second，it will lower tuition on its own summer courses to make them affordable for out-of-town students.

However，in the conversation，the woman disagrees with this announcement.

First，she says that this is too extreme because quite a few students rely on this. Not every class at every school is the same，but they could handle it. Instead，it's better to make students submit a request ahead of time，then students could find course and send in the course outline for the class they want to take. The teacher can tell students that the chemistry course didn't cover the same things and not accept it.

Second，she mentions that it will not as helpful as they think. Students still have to get housing which is a big expense while they can save money by staying at home and studying. Plus，students also want to spend time with their family and friends back home，especially after they've been away for so long.

五、Upcoming Bicycle-Riding Event

Next month，university and city officials will join together to host a weekend-long community bicycle-riding event. The goal for the event is to build more interest in biking and get more people in the community to use bicycles around town and on campus. During the weekend of the event，several downtown streets will be blocked from car traffic so that cyclists can enjoy riding their bicycles there. A map of the closed streets will be posted in advance on the university and city websites so that drivers can plan alternate routes.

1. 词汇分析1

bicycle /ˈbaɪsɪkl/　v. 骑自行车；n. 自行车

event /ɪˈvent/　n. 大事，公开活动，社交活动

build /bɪld/　n. 体格；v. 建造

interest /ˈɪntrəst/　v. 使感兴趣；n. 兴趣，利益，利息

community /kəˈmjuːnəti/　n. 社区，社团，团体

downtown /ˈdaʊnˌtaʊn/　n. 市区；adv. 在市区；adj. 闹市区的

block /blɑːk/　v. 堵塞；冻结(资金等)；n. 阻碍，块

cyclist /ˈsaɪklɪst/　n. 骑行者

post /poʊst/　　v. 邮寄，张贴

alternate /ˈɔːltərnət/　v. 交替，使交替；n. 代替者；adj. 交替的，轮流的

route /ruːt/　　n. 路线，路途

city official　市政官员

join together　一起

2. 信息提取

Next month，university and city officials will join together to host a weekend-long community bicycle-riding event.

3. 听力原文

(male student) Hey，Rita，did you see this?

(female student) Yeah，I don't think it's such a good idea. I don't think it'll have the result they're hoping for.

(male student) Why not?

(female student) Well，a lot of people are already interested now. The problem is they look around and they see that there aren't many good places to park a bike. And they're not gonna buy a bike if they know they're not gonna have any place to park it when they go out for a ride.

(male student) What do you mean?

(female student) Let's say you wanted to ride a bike downtown to do some shopping. Where would you park it while you went in the store? There are not any bike racks or any good places where you could lock up your bike and leave it while you're shopping.

(male student) You've got a point. There are many good places to park a bike on campus either now that I think of it.

(female student) Right. So what they really need to do is install lots of bike racks around the city and on the university campus. Sure, a lot more people would start riding bikes if they did that.

(male student) You're probably right.

(female student) And I know they're planning ahead for that weekend, but they're still gonna be problems.

(male student) How do you figure?

(female student) Well, you know what the city is like on the weekends. It's so busy, especially that area. A lot of people go down town to run errands. And a lot of people drive through the city on their way to other places. I'm sure the traffic will get really backed up.

(male student) Right. I see what you mean.

(female student) And not everyone who comes to the city is from around here or will think to check a website beforehand. So I just don't think it'll work. It'll definitely be a major inconvenience for a lot of people.

4. 词汇分析2

park /pɑrk/ v. 停车;n. 公园

install /ɪnˈstɔl/ v. 安装

website /ˈwebsaɪt/ n. 网站

beforehand /bɪˈfɔːrhænd/ adv. 事先

major /ˈmeɪdʒər/ adj. 主要的;n. 专业

inconvenience /ˌɪnkənˈvinɪəns/ n. 麻烦

run errand 跑腿

5. 范例答案

In the announcement, the university and city officials will join together to host a weekend-long community bicycle-riding event next month.

First, it can build more interest in biking and get more people to use bicycles.

Second, several downtown streets will be blocked from car traffic.

However, in the conversation, the woman disagrees with this announcement.

First, she says that a lot of people are already interested now, but they're not going to buy a bike because there aren't many good places to park a bike. If they ride a bike to downtown to do some shopping, there is not any bike racks or good places to lock up their bikes, which means unless they install bike racks, then a lot more people would start riding bikes.

Second, she mentions that city is busy on the weekends, especially in that area, where a lot of people go downtown to run errands. The traffic will get really backed up when people drive through the city. Plus, not everyone who comes to the city is from around here or will think to check a website beforehand. So it'll be a major inconvenience for a lot of people.

六、New Membership Requirement for Student Clubs

University spokesperson Diana Cates announced yesterday that student clubs must now have at least ten members in order to receive funding from the university. Cates said, "The university cannot justify spending money or providing facilities for such a small number of students." Regarding the new membership requirement, Cates also added, "The university feels that clubs with fewer than ten members tend not to last very long, and so we feel these clubs don't offer much benefit on students."

1. 词汇分析 1

membership /'membərʃɪp/　n. 会员

spokesperson /ˈspoʊkspɜːrsn/　*n*. 发言人

announce /əˈnaʊns/　*v*. 宣布

funding /ˈfʌndɪŋ/　*n*. 资金

justify /ˈdʒʌstɪfaɪ/　*v*. 证明；作出解释

facility /fəˈsɪləti/　*n*. 设备

offer /ˈɔːfər/　*v*. 提供；*n*. 报价，建议

benefit /ˈbenɪfɪt/　*n*. 益处；*v*. 使得益

2. 信息提取

Student clubs must now have at least ten members in order to receive funding from the university.

3. 听力原文

(female student) Hey，Robert，did you read that article about the clubs?

(male student) Yeah.

(female student) Can't believe they're gonna do this.

(male student) Would your hiking group be affected?

(female student) It's gonna be difficult for us to continue.

(male student) Oh…Sorry to hear that.

(female student) Yeah. And the reasons they give for doing it just don't make sense. I mean，the university doesn't spend that much on clubs like ours. You know，they give us enough to help pay for the admission fees to the parks where we go hiking. But that's it.

(male student) So they're not gonna save a huge amount of money.

(female student) Right! And what they spend on us is nothing compared to what they spend on other things. I mean，I'm sure they spend a lot more on bigger clubs.

(male student) Yeah，I'm sure. But，you know，I think they might have a point about what happens when there were only a few people.

(female student) Well, maybe in some cases. But we've been together for years now. And anyway, you don't have to be together for a long time to benefit from it.

(male student) How do you mean?

(female student) Well, even in a short period of time, you're gonna meet and get to know people you wouldn't have met, otherwise, people with similar interests. And that can lead a really strong friendships, lifelong connections that can help you later on in your business or your profession.

4. 词汇分析2

hiking /ˈhaɪkɪŋ/　*n*. 远足

compare /kəmˈper/　*v*. 比较

friendship /ˈfrendʃɪp/　*n*. 友谊

lifelong /ˈlaɪflɔːŋ/　*adj*. 终身的

connection /kəˈnekʃn/　*n*. 连接，关联

profession /prəˈfeʃn/　*n*. 职业，行业

admission fee　门票

a short period of time　短时间

5. 范例答案

In the announcement, the university announces that student clubs must now have at least ten members in order to receive funding from the university.

First, the university cannot justify spending money or providing facilities for such a small number of students.

Second, they believe clubs with fewer than ten members tend not to last very long, and they don't offer much benefit on students.

However, in the conversation, the woman disagrees with this announcement.

First, she says that it will be difficult for them to continue. If the university doesn't spend that much on clubs, it should give them enough to help pay for the admission fees to the parks. What they spend on small clubs like hiking club is nothing compared to what they spend on other things or bigger clubs.

Second, she mentions that their members have been together for years now, and they don't have to be together for a long time to benefit from it. Even in a short period of time, they will meet and get to know people with similar interests, which can lead to really strong friendships. She believes that lifelong connections can help later on in business or profession.

七、Open House at Campus Gym

Next week, the university will hold an open house event at the gym, in which gym staff will lead an orientation for students and give guided tours of the facility. The university hopes that this event will encourage students to exercise more regularly at the gym by providing basic instruction in how to use the exercise equipment. To motivate students to come to the open house event, those who attend will have a chance to win a $50 gift certificate to use toward athletic clothes and accessories at the campus store. At the end of the event, five students will be randomly selected to receive a $50 gift certificate.

1. 词汇分析 1

orientation /ˌɔːriənˈteɪʃn/ *n*. 方向；目标；新生见面会

encourage /ɪnˈkʌrɪdʒ/ *v*. 鼓励

regularly /ˈreɡjələli/ *adv*. 经常地；有规律地

equipment /ɪˈkwɪpmənt/ *n*. 设备

chance /tʃæns/　*n*. 机会

accessory /əkˈsesəri/　*n*. 饰品，配件

randomly /ˈrændəmli/　*adv*. 随机地

select /sɪˈlekt/　*v*. 选择

guided tour　有导游的游览

basic instruction　基本的指导

gift certificate　礼品券

athletic clothes　运动服

2. 信息提取

Next week，the university will hold an open house event at the gym，in which gym staff will lead an orientation for students and give guided tours of the facility.

3. 听力原文

(male student) Did you see this? Seems pretty cool，right?

(female student) Yeah，definitely.

(male student) I have to admit，I don't go very often. I know it's important to stay active，but I don't really know how to use all the machines.

(female student) Yeah，it can be a little intimidating. There are so many different kinds. And some of them seem sort of advanced.

(male student) Right. I mean，as a first-year student，a lot of the machines are different from what I've used before，much more complicated than what I used in high school. So that's kind of kept me from trying them.

(female student) Same here. If I knew how to use them，I think I'd go a lot more.

(male student) Right? And I'm sure a lot of students are in that situation.

(female student) Definitely.

(male student) And it's pretty cool. What they're doing is a promotion. I think it's a good idea，offering a chance or something.

(female student) And that'll work?

(male student) Oh yeah，I bet there will be a big crowd.

(female student) Yeah，I guess that's true. Students are always up for getting free stuff.

(male student) Yeah，plus it's cool to have workout clothes，a pair of sweat pants，or some T-shirts or whatever with the university logo on it.

(female student) The workout bag，gym towel. Perfect for working-out.

(male student) Exactly. Yeah. There are a lot of cool things you can get for that amount of money. Students will be excited.

4. 词汇分析2

admit /əd'mɪt/ *v.* 承认

machine /mə'ʃiːn/ *n.* 装置

intimidating /ɪn'tɪmɪdeɪtɪŋ/ *adj.* 吓人的

complicated /'kɑːmplɪkeɪtɪd/ *adj.* 复杂的

situation /ˌsɪtʃu'eɪʃn/ *n.* 情况

promotion /prə'moʊʃn/ *n.* 促进，提升

stay active 保持活跃

a big crowd 十分拥挤

workout clothes 运动服

sweat pants 运动裤

5. 范例答案

In the announcement，the university will hold an open house event at the gym，in which gym staff will lead an orientation for students and give guided tours of the facility.

First，it can encourage students to exercise more regularly at the gym.

Second, students who attend will have a chance to win a $50 gift certificate.

In the conversation, the man agrees with this announcement.

First, he says that he doesn't go very often, even if he knows it's important to stay active, he just doesn't know how to use all the machines. As a first-year student, a lot of the machines are different and much more complicated than what he used before in high school. So that has kept him from trying, and he'd go a lot more if he knows how to use them.

Second, he mentions the promotion can offer a chance for students so there will be a big crowd. It's cool to have workout clothes, a pair of sweat pants, or some T-shirts or whatever with the university logo on it. There are a lot of cool things they can get for that amount of money, so students will be excited.

八、Sporting Events Should Be Free

Sporting events like football and basketball games are an important part of college life. Unfortunately, many students don't attend games on campus because of the cost of tickets. I believe that students shouldn't have to pay for sporting events on campus. Since students already pay in order to attend the university, they shouldn't need to pay extra for tickets for these events. Making these events free for students would also help increase attendance, it is meaning that more people could go and cheer on our university's great teams.

Sincerely,

Victor Foster

1．词汇分析 1

ticket /'tɪkɪt/　n．票

extra /'ekstrə/　adv．额外；adj．额外的，附加的；n．额外的事物

increase /ɪn'kriːs/　n．增加；v．增加

attendance /ə'tendəns/　n．参加，出席

cheer /tʃɪr/　v．加油，喝彩

team /tiːm/　n．队

college life　大学生活

in order to　为了

2．信息提取

The sporting events on campus should be free.

3．听力原文

(male student) Did you see this letter?

(female student) Yeah，I did. I'm not sure it would be such a great idea.

(male student) Oh，really? Why not?

(female student) Well，for one thing，I think students would still end up paying for it. I mean，if students were not paying for the events directly，then the university would have to make the money somehow.

(male student) True.

(female student) So they probably just end up charging us all more from the beginning. When we got our bill for the semester，the bill would just be higher，you know，to help cover the cost of the games，which seems kind of unfair.

(male student) Yeah，I see what you mean. Everyone would end up paying.

（female student）Exactly! The way it is now, only people who are interested in going have to pay, which seems better to me.

（male student）Okay, that's true. But don't you think he has a point about the number of people who go to these events?

（female student）Actually, I do not think it's a problem. There are certain activities, like volleyball, maybe that might not be as popular. And maybe he's been to some of those games. But I think for most of the events, the seats tend to be full.

（male student）Yeah! The last time I tried to buy a ticket to a basketball game, they were sold out.

（female student）See what I mean? So it seems like they really don't need to encourage more people to be there. And actually, if it's totally open, there might be too many people who want to go. It could be too crowded.

4. 词汇分析 2

directly /dəˈrektli/　*adv*. 直接地

somehow /ˈsʌmhaʊ/　*adv*. 以某种方式

charge /tʃɑːrdʒ/　*n*. 充电；*v*. 收费

volleyball /ˈvɒlibɔːl/　*n*. 排球

seat /siːt/　*n*. 座位

full /fʊl/　*n*. 完全；*adj*. 满的

5. 范例答案

In the proposal, the student suggests that students shouldn't have to pay for sporting events on campus.

First, students already pay in order to attend the university.

Second, this will also help increase attendance.

However, in the conversation, the woman disagrees with this proposal.

First, she says that students would still end up paying for it. If students were not paying for the events directly, then the university would have to make up the money somehow, like charging students all more from the beginning. When they got their bill for the semester, the bill would be higher to help cover the cost of the games, which seems unfair. The present way that only people who are interested in going have to pay seems better to her.

Second, she mentions that certain activities like volleyball might not be as popular. But for most of the events, the seats tend to be full, so there's no need to encourage more people to be there. Plus, if it's totally open, there might be too many people who wanna go and it will be too crowded.

九、Virtual Campus Tours

A new feature will be available on the university website soon: a virtual campus tour. Using this feature, people will be able to experience a tour through the website, which will include photographs and videos of all university buildings and grounds. The virtual tour should benefit students who are considering applying to the university, since prospective students will not need to travel to the university to become familiar with it. The virtual tour will also highlight popular sites and well-known places to eat near campus so that current students can get information about things to do off campus.

1. 词汇分析1

feature /ˈfiːtʃər/ *n*. 特征；*v*. 以……为特色
virtual /ˈvɜːrtʃuəl/ *adj*. 几乎……的；事实上的
photograph /ˈfotəɡræf/ *n*. 照片

video /'vɪdɪo/　n．视频

ground /graʊnd/　n．土地，地面

considering /kən'sɪdərɪŋ/　prep．鉴于，考虑到，就……而言

apply /ə'plaɪ/　v．应用

prospective /prə'spektɪv/　adj．有望的，预期的

travel /'træv(ə)l/　v．旅行；n．旅行

highlight /'haɪlaɪt/　v．突出；强调；将文本的某部分用彩笔做标记

current /'kʌrənt/　n．电流，趋势，水流；adj．现在的

well-known　有名的

2．信息提取

A virtual campus tour will be available at the school website that people are able to experience a tour through it.

3．听力原文

(female student) Hey，did you see this article?

(male student) Yeah. Sounds pretty cool.

(female student) Yeah，I'm really glad they're going to do that. It makes sense because a lot of people just don't have the money or time to visit all of the schools they're thinking about applying to.

(male student) It's true. I was able to visit only a couple of the places I applied.

(female student) Well，it's especially tough if you live far away. Like，for me，as an international student，I wasn't able to visit the campus before I came here. I had to make a decision based on somewhat limited information，you know. I had seen only a few photos. So it would have been great to have a resource like this.

(male student) Yeah，that makes sense. The technology is going to be a big help.

(female student) Absolutely. It'll give people a more complete idea.

（male student）And not just about the layout of the campus，right?

（female student）Of course，That other stuff is awesome too，because sometimes all of us need a break from studying. And the newer students，especially they don't know about many places to visit when they first get here. You know，when they want to do something interesting，not related to class work.

（male student）Yeah，this will give them some good ideas like when they want to get out and just enjoy themselves，maybe go to a restaurant or go shopping.

（female student）Exactly. It'll be a little easier to learn about these places. And the new students won't feel so overwhelmed getting around when they have free time.

4．词汇分析2

glad /glæd/　adj．高兴的

international /ˌɪntərˈnæʃnəl/　adj．国际的

limited /ˈlɪmɪtɪd/　adj．限制的

resource /rɪˈsɔːs/　n．资料

complete /kəmˈpliːt/　adj．完全的；v．完成

awesome /ˈɔːsəm/　adj．令人惊叹的

overwhelm /ˌoʊvərˈwelm/　v．淹没

far away　远的

make a decision　做决定

5．范例答案

In the announcement，the university website will soon have a virtual campus tour.

First，prospective students will not need to travel to the university to become familiar with it.

Second，it can highlight popular sites and well-known places to eat near campus.

In the conversation，the woman agrees with this announcement.

First, she says that a lot of people don't have the money or time to visit all of the schools they're applying to, especially tough if they live far away. Like she wasn't able to visit the campus before as an international student, so she had to make a decision based on limited information, seeing only a few photos. Therefore, the website resource will be great.

Second, she mentions that technology can give people a more complete idea and that would be awesome, since sometimes students need a break from studying. For example, newer students usually don't know about many places to visit when they first arrive. When they wanna do something interesting and not related to class work, it'll be easier to learn about these places. And the new students won't feel so overwhelmed getting around when they have free time.

十、Classes to Begin Later

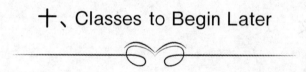

The university has announced that, beginning next year, the first classes of the day will start an hour later, at 9 am, instead of 8 am. The change comes in response to the frequent complaints of professors that students are too sleepy to concentrate and to participate in class discussions in early morning classes. The university hopes that the extra hour will help students come to class with better rest and more ready to learn. The change will also provide professors with more time at the beginning of the working day to prepare for their classes.

1. 词汇分析 1

response /rɪˈspɑːns/ *n*. 回应
frequent /ˈfriːkwənt/ *adj*. 频繁的

complaint /kəmˈpleɪnt/　*n*. 投诉,抱怨

sleepy /ˈslipi/　*adj*. 困的

concentrate /ˈkɑːnsntreɪt/　*v*. 集中

participate /pɑːrˈtɪsɪpeɪt/　*v*. 参加

discussion /dɪˈskʌʃ(ə)n/　*n*. 讨论

prepare /prɪˈper/　*v*. 准备

working day　工作日

2. 信息提取

Beginning next year, the first classes of the day will start an hour later, at 9 am, instead of 8 am.

3. 听力原文

(male student)Hey, did you see this article?

(female student)Yeah, I did I think it's a great idea, don't you?

(male student)Well, actually no. I kind of prefer to get an early start, and anyway, I don't think it will have the effect on students as they think it will.

(female student)What do you mean?

(male student)Well, the thing is when students know they have more time they'll probably just stay up later at night. I don't think their sleeping habits will really change much.

(female student)Yeah, I see your point.

(male student)I mean unless it's much later in the morning, there will still be a lot of students who didn't get enough sleep. It's just what happens, college students don't always make the best decisions about how much sleep they need at night. They like to stay up late working on assignments or hanging out with friends or whatever.

(female student)So it may not make that much of a difference.

（male student）Right! And I don't think it will help the professors that much either.

（female student）Why not?

（male student）Well，because a lot of them have to drive quite a distance to get to the university and the traffic is actually worse at that time of day since that's when most people are going to work.

（female student）Yeah，I guess there can be lots of cars out on the road then.

（male student）Exactly，so it will end up taking them longer to drive here，which means they won't really benefit from that. Extra time will probably just end up spending more time in their cars.

（female student）I hadn't thought of that.

（male student）Yeah，so I wish they'd just leave things the way they are.

4. 词汇分析2

habit /ˈhæbɪt/ n. 习惯

assignment /əˈsaɪnmənt/ n. 任务，作业

distance /ˈdɪstəns/ n. 距离；v. 拉开距离，与······疏远

traffic /ˈtræfɪk/ n. 路上行驶的车辆；交通

benefit /ˈbenɪfɪt/ n. 好处；v. 得益于

have the effect on 对······有影响

stay up 熬夜

hang out 闲逛

end up 最后

5. 范例答案

In the announcement，the university announces that beginning next year，the first classes of the day will start an hour later，at 9 am，instead of 8 am. Because first，it will give students an extra one hour to have a better rest. Also，professors will have more time to prepare for their classes.

However, in the conversation, the man disagrees with this announcement.

First, he says that, if students have more time, they might stay up later at night. It will not change their sleeping habits. So they will not get enough sleep. Many college students like to stay up late for assignments or hang out with friends.

Also, he mentions that as for professors, many of them drive to campus. And at that time the traffic is really worse, because that's when most people go to work. So it might finally take them longer to get to university.

十一、New Government Internship Program

Starting this year, political science and economics students may apply to spend a summer in the state's capital city and complete an internship with the state government, working in a government office. The political science department decided to create this internship program so that students will have the opportunity to gain work experience that will help prepare them for future careers working for the government. In order to ensure that selected interns are academically prepared for the internship, only students who have completed two years of coursework in either the political science or economics department will be eligible to apply for this program.

1. 词汇分析1

internship /'ɪntɜːnˌʃɪp/   n. 实习
government /'gʌvərnmənt/   n. 政府
gain /geɪn/   v. 获得
future /'fjuːtʃə/   n. 未来

intern /ˈɪntɜːn/　*n*. 实习生

academically /ˌækəˈdemɪkəlɪ/　*adv*. 学术上地

coursework /ˈkɔːrsəwɜːk/　*n*. 课程作业

eligible /ˈelɪdʒəbl/　*adj*. 有资格的

capital city　首都

political science　政治学

2. 信息提取

Starting this year, political science and economics students may apply to spend a summer to complete an internship with the state government.

3. 听力原文

(male student) Hey, you're studying political science, right? Did you see this?

(female student) Yeah, I think it looks like a really good opportunity, it could really help students when they were looking for jobs after graduation. You know, not just because of the work itself, but also think about the people you would meet.

(male student) Are other people working there?

(female student) Yeah exactly. My professors have told me that for these kinds of jobs, it's really important to make connections with other people in the field.

(male student) Oh, that makes sense.

(female student) Right. So this would be a really good way to start meeting people. You'd get to work with them and get to know them and feel comfortable asking them questions about their experiences at work, whether they have any advice. You might even stay in touch with them afterwards.

(male student) That does sound helpful, but it's not open to everyone you know.

(female student) Well, that makes a lot of sense to me.

(male student) Yeah?

(female student) Yeah，I am sure they will expect you to have a certain amount of background knowledge when you start.

(male student) I guess that would probably help.

(female student) Of course you're going to learn a lot that. You're not expected to know everything right away，but they'll expect you to have a solid foundation. You already know basic things，about how the government functions，so that you will understand the purpose of the work you are being asked to do.

(male student) That seems reasonable.

4．词汇分析 2

graduation /ˌɡrædʒuˈeɪʃn/　n．毕业

connection /kəˈnekʃn/　n．连接

field /fiːld/　n．领域

afterward /ˈæftərwərd/　adv．后来

solid /ˈsɑːlɪd/　n．固体；adj．固体的

foundation /faʊnˈdeɪʃ(ə)n/　n．基础

function /ˈfʌŋkʃn/　n．功能；v．起作用

purpose /ˈpɜːrpəs/　n．目的

reasonable /ˈriːznəbl/　adj．讲得通的

stay in touch with　与……保持联系

5．范例答案

The university announces that starting this year，political science and economics students may apply to complete an internship with the state government. Because first，it will help students gain work experience.

Second，only students who have completed two years of coursework in either of those two departments are eligible to apply for it.

However, in the conversation, the woman disagrees with this announcement.

First, she says it can really help students to look for a job after graduation. Because they can meet many people, and make connections with the people in the field. Like students can work with them and ask them questions about their experiences at work. They might even offer some advice.

Also, she mentions that it is necessary for students to have some backgrounds, because students need to have a solid foundation. They already know basic things, like how the government functions, so they can understand the purpose, when they are asked to do something.

第十四章　Task 3

一、Dormancy

During periods when climate conditions are extremely harsh and food and water are scarce，some animals survive by entering into a state of inactivity，known as dormancy：the animal takes measures to avoid exposure to the elements，and its bodily processes slow down. Because dormant animals are not physically active，they have little need for nourishment. They can，therefore，remain in a dormant state for long periods of time until more favorable environmental conditions return.

1. 词汇分析 1

climate /ˈklaɪmət/　*n*. 气候

condition /kənˈdɪʃn/　*n*. 状况，状态；条件，环境

harsh /hɑːrʃ/　*adj*. (环境)恶劣的，艰苦的

scarce /skers/　*adj*. 缺乏的，不足的

inactivity /ˌɪnækˈtɪvɪti/　*n*. 不活动，静止，休止状态

exposure /ɪkˈspoʊʒər/　*n*. 暴露，接触；曝光

nourishment /ˈnɜːrɪʃmənt/　*n*. 滋养品，营养

favorable /ˈfeɪvərəbl/　*adj.* 有利的；良好的

take measures to　采取措施

2. 信息提取

Dormancy is a phenomenon that animals survive by entering into a state of inactivity in extreme climate conditions.

3. 听力原文

A good example of this is a type of fish that lives in Australia and Africa called lungfish. Lungfish live in shallow lakes and during the summer when it's very hot and dry, the lakes dry up. Now how can a fish possibly survive in a dried up lake that's being cooked by the sun all day long. Well, as the dry season approaches before the water is completely dried up, the lungfish digs itself down into a hole in the mud at the bottom of the lake. So it's buried in the mud.

And what it does is it curls itself up and covers itself with slime and mud. It forms a sort of protective code of slime and mud. It protects the fish from heat and helps keep it moist. And during this time it remains very still and it's breathing slows down to where it's breathing only maybe once or twice per hour. And its heart slows down to where it's beating only about three times per minute and it remains very still.

Now normally the lungfish eats fish, crabs and other meaty things, but when the lakes dried up like this, its food supply isn't available. But that's OK because in this state the lungfish is burning very little energy. So it doesn't need to eat. In fact, it can stay safe in its protected shelter without food and use very little energy for months even years if necessary while it waits for the rains to return.

4. 词汇分析 2

shallow /ˈʃæloʊ/ *adj*. 浅的,不深的;*n*.(海、湖或河的)浅水处,浅滩

approach /əˈproʊtʃ/ *v*. 靠近,处理;*n*. 方法,态度

dig /dɪg/ *v*. 搜寻,寻找;挖,掘

mud /mʌd/ *n*. 泥,淤泥,泥浆

slime /slaɪm/ *n*. 黏液;烂泥

shelter /ˈʃeltər/ *n*. 居所,住处,遮蔽物

curl up 卷起

dried up 干涸的

5. 范例答案

According to the reading, dormancy is a phenomenon that animals survive by entering into a state of inactivity in extreme climate conditions.

In the lecture, the professor gives an example of lungfish. Lungfish lives in shallow lakes and during the summer when it's very hot and dry, the lakes dry up. Before the water is completely dried up, the lungfish digs itself down into a hole in the mud at the bottom of the lake. So it's buried in the mud.

And then it curls itself up and covers itself with slime and mud. It forms a sort of protective code, which protects the fish from heat and helps keep it moist. And during this time it remains very still and it's breathing only maybe once or twice per hour. At the same time, its heart slows down to where it's beating only about three times per minute.

Normally the lungfish eats fish, crabs and other meaty things, but when the lakes dried up like this, its food supply isn't available. But that's OK because in this way the lungfish doesn't need to eat for months even years.

二、Evolutionary Loss

Over time，plant and animal species adapt in response to their environments and may develop new features that are helpful in those environments. However，evolution can also involve the loss of certain features. This is known as evolutionary loss. Evolutionary loss is observed in modern members of a species when they no longer have a feature that their ancestors once had. This often occurs because a species has moved to a new environment. The once-useful feature may no longer be helpful or even necessary in the new environment and therefore diminishes over successive generations，until it eventually disappears entirely.

1. 词汇分析 1

feature /ˈfiːtʃər/　n．特征

evolution /ˌiːvəˈluːʃn/　n．进化

environment /ɪnˈvaɪrənmənt/　n．环境

loss /lɔːs/　n．损失

ancestor /ˈænsestər/　n．祖先

involve /ɪnˈvɑːlv/　v．包括

adapt /əˈdæpt/　v．适应

diminish /dɪˈmɪnɪʃ/　v．削弱

successive generation　连续的后代

in response to　为了应对

2. 信息提取

Evolutionary loss is observed in modern members of a species when they no longer have a feature that their ancestors once had.

3. 听力原文

Now, listen to part of a lecture from a biology class.

So, an interesting example of this can be seen in a small insect called the ice crawler, which as you might guess from the name, it lives in cold areas. And crawlers, they crawl around since they don't have wings and can't fly. But the ice crawler didn't always live in cold climates. In fact, millions of years ago these insects lived in warm tropical forests, and they had a different way of getting around. They had wings which allowed them to fly around from plant to plant, feeding on pollen from the flowers.

Now, for a while there was relatively little competition for pollen, but at a certain point, more and more insects started living in these tropical forests as well, making it difficult for all the insects to get enough food, so here's where it gets kind of interesting. Because the tropical forests became so crowded with other insects, overtime, some insects, like the ancestors of ice crawlers, left these areas, eventually settling in cold icy areas. There, in these cold environments there wasn't really competition for food. The ice crawlers didn't need to get around from flower to flower anymore collecting pollen, because they could easily find dead leaves and other debris on the ground, in the ice and snow.

And another important thing, flying requires a lot of energy, the ice crawlers needed to stay warm enough to survive in this new icy environment. And so overtime, well, that's why ice crawlers look a lot different today than they did millions of years ago.

Explain how the example from the lecture illustrates the concept of evolutionary loss.

4. 词汇分析2

insect /ˈɪnsekt/　　*n*. 昆虫

climate /ˈklaɪmət/　　*n*. 气候

pollen /ˈpɑːlən/　　*n*. 花粉

competition /ˌkɑːmpəˈtɪʃn/　　*n*. 竞争

debris /dəˈbriː/　　*n*. 残骸

energy /ˈenərdʒi/　　*n*. 能量

crowded /ˈkraʊdɪd/　　*adj*. 拥挤的

crawl /krɔːl/　　*v*. 爬行

require /rɪˈkwaɪr/　　*v*. 需要

tropical forest　　热带森林

5. 范例答案

According to the reading, evolutionary loss is observed in modern members of a species when they no longer have a feature that their ancestors once had.

In the lecture, the professor gives an example of an insect called ice crawler to illustrate it. It lives in cold areas and crawl around since they don't have wings and can't fly. But in fact, millions of years ago, ice crawlers lived in warm tropical forests, and they had wings fly around from plant to plant, feeding on pollen from the flowers.

But with more and more insects lived in the forests, it is difficult to get enough food. So the ancestors of ice crawlers left there, and eventually settled in cold icy areas, because there wasn't really competition for food. And the ice crawlers didn't need to fly to collect pollen, because they could easily find dead leaves and other debris on the ground.

And also, flying requires a lot of energy that the ice crawlers needed to stay warm enough to survive in the icy environment. So, overtime, ice crawlers look a lot differently.

三、Transitional Forms

Modern animal species are descended from other，earlier species，but these prehistoric species did not change into their modern forms all at once. Some scientists theorize that these animals first went through intermediary or transitional forms. Transitional forms of animals are animals that lived between the time of their ancestors and that of the modern species that we are familiar with today. They had acquired some of the characteristics and physical features of their modern-day descendants but still retained certain physical features of the older animal species from which they had evolved. Transitional forms are important because they help scientists to understand how different animal species evolved.

1. 词汇分析 1

acquire /əˈkwaɪər/　*v*. 获得

theorize /ˈθɪəraɪz/　*v*. 理论化

remain /rɪˈmeɪn/　*v*. 剩余, 保留

evolve /iˈvɑːlv/　*v*. 进化

species /ˈspiːʃiːz/　*n*. 物种

ancestor /ˈænsestər/　*n*. 祖先

characteristics /ˌkærɪktəˈrɪstɪks/　*n*. 特征

descendant /dɪˈsendənt/　*n*. 后代

intermediary /ˌɪntərˈmiːdieri/　*n*. 中间阶段

transitional /trænˈzɪʃənl/　*adj*. 过渡的

physical feature　生物特征

prehistoric species　史前物种

2．信息提取

Transitional forms of animals are animals that lived between the time of their ancestors and that of the modern species that we are familiar with today.

3．听力原文

Now，listen to part of a lecture from a biology class.

Okay. Let's see an example of this. So，millions of years ago，there were ancient fish living in the water but no animals on land. Animals had not come out of the water and started living on land yet，and there's one particular kind of fish from that time period that is a good example of this phenomenon.

Now this particular fish lived a very long time ago，but there have been other fish that lived before and just like all the other fish before it had done，this fish breathed with gills. You know，it could use its gills to breathe in water. At the same time，however，this fish had some of the same bone structures as the land animals that would evolve from it over the course of millions of years. Why? Well，this fish lived in shallow water，close to land. Although the fish had fins，just like other fish，it has special bones in its fins that made them strong enough to support its weight. Scientists think that the fish used these strong fins，a little like land animals use their legs. The fins have the same bone structure as the legs of later land animals，and the fish could use the fins to move themselves along the bottom of the shallow water and look for food.

Explain how the example in the lecture illustrates the concept of transitional forms.

4．词汇分析 2

ancient /ˈenʃənt/　*adj*. 古时的，古代的

particular /pərˈtɪkjələr/ *adj.* 特殊的

shallow /ˈʃæləʊ/ *adj.* 浅的

period /ˈpɪrɪəd/ *n.* 阶段

phenomenon /fəˈnɑːmɪnən/ *n.* 现象

gill /dʒɪl/ *n.* 鳃

fin /fɪn/ *n.* 鳍

breathe /briːθ/ *v.* 呼吸

support /səˈpɔːrt/ *v.* 支撑

land animal 陆地动物

bone structure 骨骼结构

5. 范例答案

According to the reading, transitional forms of animals are animals that lived between the time of their ancestors and that of the modern species that we are familiar with today.

In the lecture, the professor gives an example of a fish to illustrate it. This particular fish lived a very long time ago, just like all the other fish before it, this fish breathed with gills. At the same time, however, this fish had some of the same bone structures as the land animals because this fish lived in shallow water, close to land. Although the fish had fins, just like other fish, it also has special bones in its fins that made them strong enough to support its weight. Scientists think that it used these strong fins, like land animals use their legs. The fins have the same bone structure as the legs of later land animals, and the fish could use the fins to move themselves along the bottom of the shallow water and look for food.

四、Flipped Classroom

With traditional teaching methods，teachers use class time to lecture and introduce new information to students. Students then perform the challenging task of applying the new information by completing assignments outside of class without assistance from the teacher. Research has shown，however，that students may learn better when traditional methods are reversed and teachers instead use the flipped classroom method. Using this method，teachers often record lectures for students to listen to on their own outside of class. This makes class time available for students to complete the more challenging task of applying the new information from the lecture by working on assignments in class with guidance from the teacher.

1. 词汇分析 1

assignment /əˈsaɪnmənt/   n. 任务

assistance /əˈsɪstəns/   n. 帮助

guidance /ˈgaɪdns/   n. 引导

method /ˈmeθəd/   n. 方法

perform /pərˈfɔːrm/   v. 表现

record /ˈrekərd/   v. 记录

apply /əˈplaɪ/   v. 应用

traditional /trəˈdɪʃənl/   adj. 传统的

reserved /rɪˈzɜːrvd/   adj. 逆转的

challenging /ˈtʃælɪndʒɪŋ/   adj. 有挑战的

available /əˈveɪləbl/   adj. 可用的

teaching method　*教学方法*

2. 信息提取

Flipped classroom is a teaching method that teachers record lectures for students to listen to on their own outside of class.

3. 听力原文

Now, listen to part of a lecture on this topic from an education class.

Okay, so I have a friend who's a high school math teacher and she started doing this recently.

Before, if there was a new math concept for the students to learn, she'd explained it in class and then gave her students problems to work on at home in order to learn the new concept. But she noticed that a lot of times when the kids turned their assignments in the next day, they made lots of mistakes, or maybe they'd gotten stuck and not finished all the problems because they did not understand or weren't sure how to do the work. So she decided to try something different.

Now when there's a new math concept for students to learn, she makes a video of herself explaining the concept and she posts the video online so that all the students can watch the video on the internet from home, using their own computers to learn about the new concept. Then, the next day my friend gives the students a set of problems to work on in class. Problems based on the concept she posted the video about. And while the students are working on the problems, she's able to go around the classroom and answer their questions while they're doing the problems. So if someone's not sure how to solve a problem, she can help them right away and she says this has really helped her students. They've been doing much better on the quizzes and tests she gives them.

Explain how the example from the lecture illustrates the flipped classroom method.

4. 词汇分析2

concept /ˈkɑːnsept/　*n*. 概念

quiz /kwɪz/　*n*. 测试

explain /ɪkˈspleɪn/　*v*. 解释

post /pəʊst/　*v*. 上传

solve /sɑːlv/　*v*. 解决

online /ˌɑːnˈlaɪn/　*adj*. 线上的

turn in　上交

base on　根据

get stuck　卡住

5. 范例答案

According to the reading，flipped classroom is a teaching method that teachers record lectures for students to listen to on their own outside of class.

In the lecture，the professor gives an example of a math teacher to illustrate it. Before，she would explain the new math concept in class and gave students problems to work on at home. But she noticed when they turned assignments in，there were lots of mistakes，or they could not finish all the problems because they did not understand or weren't sure how to do them.

So，now she would record herself explaining the concept and post it online so that students can watch it from home，and use computers to learn. Then，the next day she gives the students problems about the concept to work on，And she's able to go around the classroom and answer the questions. So if someone's not sure how to solve a problem，she can help them right away and this really helped the students. They do much better on the quizzes and tests.

五、Eminent Domain

When a government wants to complete a large public project that will benefit many people，it sometimes becomes necessary for the government to take control of private property that belongs to private citizens. This governmental power is known as eminent domain. Under most eminent domain laws，individual property owners are reimbursed or paid for the value of their property that is taken. Even though a government's practice of eminent domain can be a disturbance for people whose property is taken，the law allows governments to complete public projects that are advantageous for society as a whole.

1. 词汇分析1

government /ˈɡʌvərnmənt/　*n*. 政府

property /ˈprɑːpərti/　*n*. 财产

citizen /ˈsɪtɪzn/　*n*. 市民

disturbance /dɪˈstɜːrbəns/　*n*. 干扰

private /ˈpraɪvət/　*adj*. 私人的

advantageous /ˌædvənˈteɪdʒəs/　*adj*. 有利的

reimburse /ˌriːɪmˈbɜːrs/　*v*. 偿还

public project　公共项目

eminent domain　征用土地

take control of　控制

2. 信息提取

Eminent domain is the governmental power to take control of private property that belongs to private citizens.

3. 听力原文

Now, listen to part of a lecture from a political science class.

So, this happens more often than you might think. In California, there is a good example of this, where the state government took some land in order to build a railroad. Why? Well, you see, there was just one major highway there that connected two large cities and that meant that there was a lot of traffic congestion on the road. And this was a problem, particularly because so many trucks use the road to transport goods back and forth and that was being slowed down because of all the traffic.

So the government stepped in and decided to build a railroad through the area, because train would reduce the amount of traffic on the road and make it faster for people and goods to travel between the two cities. The problem was, the railroad would have to cut across a lot of privately owned land. I know about this because my uncle was one of the people who would have to give up his land for them to build the railroad.

Now, they had a legal right to take my uncle's land and they offered him a lot of money to buy it from him, but he wasn't happy about it. He lived there all his life and didn't want to move. But, well, he really didn't have any choice. He had to follow the law, so he gave up his land and took the money.

Now that they finish the railroad though, he says that it was worth it. He sees that the train really did benefit the whole community, since there aren't many traffic problems anymore and people don't have to wait to get the things they need.

Explain how the example from the lecture illustrates the concept of eminent domain.

4. 词汇分析2

railroad /ˈreɪlrəʊd/　n. 铁路

highway /ˈhaɪweɪ/　n. 高速公路

community /kəˈmjuːnəti/　n. 社区

truck /trʌk/　n. 卡车

connect /kəˈnekt/　v. 联系，连接

transport /ˈtrænspɔːrt/　v. 运输

legal right　合法权利

give up　放弃

step in　介入

back and forth　来回

traffic congestion　交通堵塞

5. 范例答案

According to the reading, eminent domain is the governmental power to take control of private property that belongs to private citizens.

In the lecture, the professor gives an example of building railroad to illustrate it. In California, there was just one major highway connecting two large cities and was a lot of traffic congestion, which slowed down the transport. So government decided to build a railroad to reduce the amount of traffic and make it faster to travel. But the problem was the railroad had to cut across a lot of private land. Professor's uncle owned one of them and had to give up his land.

It's legal to take the land and they offered a lot of money to his uncle. But he was not happy because he didn't want to move. However, he didn't have choice and followed the law. So he gave up and took the money.

Now he thinks it was worth because it benefits the whole community. There are not so much traffic and people don't need to wait to get things.

六、Maturation Effect

Researchers often design studies to evaluate the effectiveness of new products or programs. When conducting such a study and analyzing its results，it is important for researchers to consider the natural physical or mental developments that the study participants may undergo during the course of the study，because these developments can lead to a maturation effect. Participants may undergo physical and mental changes unrelated to the program being tested，which can cause the results of the study to be flawed and unusable. The program may appear to be effective，when in fact participants' naturally occurring physical and mental developments are partly responsible for the results.

1. 词汇分析 1

evaluate /ɪˈvæljueɪt/　v．评估

conduct /kənˈdʌkt/　v．实施,进行

analyze /ˈænəlaɪz/　v．分析

undergo /ˌʌndərˈgoʊ/　v．经历

maturation /ˌmætʃuˈreɪʃn/　n．成熟

participant /pɑːrˈtɪsɪpənt/　n．参与者

effectiveness /ɪˈfektɪvnəs/　n．有效性

flawed /flɔːd/　adj．有误的

unusable /ˌʌnˈjuːzəbl/　adj．无法使用的

responsible /rɪˈspɑːnsəbl/　adj．负责任的

physical and mental development 身心发展

2. 信息提取

Maturation effect means that participants may undergo physical and mental changes unrelated to the program being tested，which can cause the results of the study to be flawed and unusable.

3. 听力原文

Now，listen to part of a lecture in a psychology class.

Okay，so here's a classic example of this. Say a fitness organization wants to create an exercise routine for teenagers to help them improve their strength and get stronger，and the fitness organization wants to know if their routine is actually going to work，so they conduct a study.

The researchers start by testing a small group of teenagers to see how strong they are，and then they have the teens do these exercises a few times a week for a year，to try and build strength. And at the end of the year，they tested teenagers again to see how strong they are after they've been doing the exercises. And what do they find? Well，they find that the teens have indeed gotten a lot stronger over the course of the year. So that sounds good，the exercise routine works，right?

But the thing is，over the course of a year，most teenagers grow quite a bit，as you'd expect，teenage years are a pretty intense period of growth. And so as these teens grew，their muscles developed and they naturally got stronger. So at the end of this study，what can the researchers say about the effectiveness of the exercise routine? Not really a whole lot，right? It would be hard to say whether or not the teens' strength actually increased because of the exercise routine.

Explain how the example from the lecture illustrates the maturation effect.

4. 词汇分析 2

classic /ˈklæsɪk/　*adj*. 经典的

intense /ɪnˈtens/　*adj*. 强烈的,剧烈的

routine /ruːˈtiːn/　*n*. 日常

strength /streŋkθ/　*n*. 力量

muscle /ˈmʌsl/　*n*. 肌肉

growth /grəʊθ/　*n*. 增长

conduct a study　进行研究

fitness organization　健身机构

5. 范例答案

According to the reading, maturation effect means that participants may undergo physical and mental changes unrelated to the program being tested, which can cause the results of the study to be flawed and unusable.

In the lecture, the professor gives an example — an exercise study to illustrate it. A fitness organization wants to create an exercise routine for teenagers to help them improve strength and get stronger, and they want to know if their routine is working. So, they test a small group of teenagers to see how strong they are, and then the teens need to do these exercises a few times a week for a year. At the end of the year, they test teenagers again to see how strong they are. As a result, the teens have become stronger, and the exercise routine seems to work.

But actually, during the year, most teenagers grow, as teenage years are an intense period of growth. Their muscles developed and they naturally got stronger. So it would be hard to say whether or not the teens' strength increased because of the exercise routine.

七、Mass Customization

Sometimes consumers want products to be customized，or specifically designed to meet their individual needs. However，customize products can be expensive and time consuming for companies to make. Thus，many companies use an approach called mass customization to satisfy consumers' desire for customized products. With this approach，a company produces large quantities of a standard product，which has some interchangeable components or parts that consumers can choose to meet their specific needs. While this approach provides consumers with customized products，companies also benefit from keeping the manufacturing process efficient and costs low.

1. 词汇分析1

customize /ˈkʌstəmaɪz/ v. 定制，量身定制

individual /ˌɪndɪˈvɪdʒuəl/ adj. 个人的；个别的

satisfy /ˈsætɪsfaɪ/ v. 满足

standard /ˈstændərd/ adj. 标准的

interchangeable /ˌɪntərˈtʃeɪndʒəbl/ adj. 可交换的，可替换的

component /kəmˈpoʊnənt/ n. 成分

approach /əˈproʊtʃ/ n. 方法；v. 接近

2. 信息提取

Mass customization is an approach that a company produces large quantities of a standard product，which has some interchangeable components that consumers can choose to meet their specific needs.

3. 听力原文

OK，so let's consider an example of this. We see this with computers，so you know people have been buying computers for a while now，but in the earlier days，it was basically the same computer for everyone who wanted one. But none of the big computer companies recognize that people use computers for different things. Not everyone had the same needs. So this company allowed customers to make a limited number of choices about the computer they bought. Things like，they could select the amount of memory in the computer，the size of the screen，and whether they wanted the computer to have a disk drive. With this，customers could get what they wanted in their computers. So while the company gave customers their choice of computers，they could still make lots of this same computer and the basic frame was the same. And the computer company had all the parts ready. So it was easy to assemble the particular machine the customer wanted，and send the finished computer out to the customer. And since the company didn't have to start from scratch to make a computer for each customer，the computers were relatively cheap. So lots of people bought them，and the company did well better than other computer companies at the time.

4. 词汇分析2

recognize /ˈrekəgnaɪz/   v. 识别，认识
disk drive （计算机）磁盘驱动器
start from scratch 从头开始

5. 范例答案

In the reading, mass customization is an approach that a company produces large

quantities of a standard product，which has some interchangeable components that consumers can choose to meet their specific needs.

In the lecture，the professor gives an example of selling computer to explain it. Back to earlier period，most computers were basically the same in the market.

But a big company started to set up different things since not everyone had the same needs. It allowed limited choices for customers，like select the amount of memory，size of the screen，and even whether to own a disk drive.

Meanwhile，it also made lots of same computers with basic frame. And it was easy to send the finished basic computer. Since the company didn't have to start from scratch，it was cheaper to buy computers.

So more people wanted to buy and the company did much better than others.

八、Open Source Development

Many companies restrict access to the designs of their products in order to protect them from their competitors，so that those competitors do not copy their products. Sometimes，however，companies may encourage all interested people to access and modify their designs，even if these people are from a competing company. This model of development，known as open source development，allows companies to work together cooperatively to improve products. This model can be beneficial when products require new technology that is expensive and complex，since companies can share costs and work together to find solutions to problems in order to create successful products.

1. 词汇分析1

competitor /kəmˈpetɪtər/ *n*. 竞争者

modify /ˈmɑːdɪfaɪ/　*v*. 修改

restrict /rɪˈstrɪkt/　*v*. 限制

access /ˈækses/　*v*. 获取，进入，访问

cooperative /koʊˈɑːpərətɪv/　*adj*. 合作的

2. 信息提取

Open source development refers to a model to encourage all interested people to access and modify their designs, even if these people are from a competing company.

3. 听力原文

So, there's a small car company that did this recently. It makes these electric cars, the cars that don't use gasoline, but run on batteries instead. Well when the company was just a few years old, it was struggling. It wasn't selling very many of these cars. Why? Well, the cars were incredibly expensive to make, and to be honest they didn't work very well. Electric cars require batteries that are both light weight and able to hold a lot of electricity. At the time batteries like that didn't really exist. So the company had research and spend a lot of money trying to design them. So the cars weren't very efficient at first, and the cost of trying to make them more efficient got added to the price of the cars. Well, this company decided to do an unusual thing. They announced that they would make the designs for their batteries available to other car companies. And instead of being bad for the company, it turned out very well. The other companies had some good ideas about ways to make the batteries cheaper and more efficient. All of the companies started selling cars with the improved batteries. And since the cars were better designed and less expensive overall, all of the companies sold more electric cars than ever before.

4．词汇分析2

incredibly /ɪnˈkredəbli/　*adv*．难以置信地，非常地

battery /ˈbætəri/　*n*．电池

electric /ɪˈlektrɪk/　*adj*．电动的，电的

announce /əˈnaʊns/　*v*．宣布，公告

5．范例答案

In the reading，open source development refers to a model to encourage all interested people to access and modify their designs，even if these people are from a competing company.

In the lecture，the professor gives an example of a car company to explain it. Previously，a company had the idea of electric car by running on batteries. But at first，it was struggling to sell since it was expensive to make：it required both light weight and large amount of battery holding，which didn't exist at that time.

Then the company decided unusually to announce this idea available for other companies. And it went well since other companies presented good ways of designing it cheaper and more efficient.

In the end，all the companies improved the batteries，so the cars were less expensive and caused more deals.

九、Environmental Impact Assessment

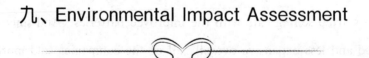

The construction of a new building affects the natural environment in a number of ways. In order to minimize effects that could be negative，the consequences of any construction project must be considered before construction of a new building begins. Using a process called environmental impact assessment，the planners of a construction project assess or evaluate the effects that it would have on the environment. If this assessment indicates that the proposed construction project would be bad for the environment in some way，the project planners may need to adjust the construction plan.

1. 词汇分析 1

construction /kənˈstrʌkʃn/　n. 建造

minimize /ˈmɪnɪmaɪz/　v. 最小化

consequence /ˈkɑːnsɪkwens/　n. 结果

evaluate /ɪˈvæljueɪt/　v. 评价

assessment /əˈsesmənt/　n. 评估

indicate /ˈɪndɪkeɪt/　v. 指出，表明

2. 信息提取

Environmental impact assessment means that the planners of a construction project assess or evaluate the effects that it would have on the environment.

3. 听力原文

Ok，so，for example，let's say a construction company is planning to build a shopping center on a large piece of land. Before starting the project，the construction company does some research and makes a study of the area，and they learn that the area where they plan to build the shopping center is a wetland，you know，a soft marshy area where there is lots of water in the soil. They plan to bring in additional soil to fill in the area to make the ground more solid and firm so they can build on it. But what effect might this, filling in of the wetland, have on the area? Well, the construction company finds out that the wetland is actually very important to the region, the wetlands is helpful in preventing flooding in the surrounding area. You see, a wetland holds a lot of water. The soil is very absorbent, so by absorbing and holding extra rainwater the wetland functions in a beneficial way, it actually reduces the chance of flooding in the area. So the construction company, if it filled in the wetlands and then built the shopping center on it, the wetland would be destroyed. Well, they can't do that, right? So the construction company decides to cancel their original plan, instead they moved the entire shopping center project to a different location.

4. 词汇分析 2

wetland /ˈwetlənd/　*n*. 沼泽地,湿地

marshy /ˈmɑːrʃi/　*adj*. 沼泽的

solid /ˈsɑːlɪd/　*adj*. 牢固的

absorbent /əbˈzɔːrbənt/　*adj*. 能吸收的

5. 范例答案

In the reading, environmental impact assessment means that the planners of a construction project assess or evaluate the effects that it would have on the environment.

In the lecture, the professor elaborates on it by an example of a construction company. At first, this company planned to build a shopping center in an area. Before doing it, the company did some research and found out it was a wetland in this area. So the company planned to fill in additional soil in the area to build.

However, the company figured it would affect the environment. The wetland could prevent the flood since it could hold the extra rain water in absorbance. So the company's construction would actually destroy the area.

As a result, the company canceled the plan and chose another area.

十、Effort Justification

People do not like to admit to themselves and others that they have wasted effort on something that is unimportant. Therefore, if people work hard to attain or accomplish something, they tend to subconsciously justify or defend the effort they made, so that it seems worthwhile. This is known as effort justification. Because of effort justification, when people are required to exert significant effort to achieve or gain access to something, they tend to place a higher value on that accomplishment than if they were to attain it with little effort. Regardless of the actual attributes of the achievement, simply having worked hard for it makes it seem more valuable in the person's mind.

1. 词汇分析 1

admit /əd'mɪt/　v. 承认

subconsciously /ˌsʌb'kɒnʃəsli/　adv. 潜意识地

justify /'dʒʌstɪfaɪ/　v. 合理化

attributes /ə'trɪbjuːts/　n. 属性

attain /ə'teɪn/　v. 获得，实现，达到

2. 信息提取

Effort justification means that if people work hard to attain or accomplish something, they tend to subconsciously justify or defend the effort they made, so that it seems worthwhile.

3. 听力原文

Okay, so let me tell you about an experiment I tried out with one of my classes a few years back that demonstrated this. So I told my class that I was going to hold a special discussion group, in which we watch a movie and talk about it afterwards. I made joining the group sounds like kind of a privilege and explained that whoever was interested would have to complete and pass an assignment first to understood different psychological concepts. Okay. So then I took all the students who said they'd be interested in joining the discussion group, and I divided them up. Now for the assignment, half of the students had to answer a bunch of really easy questions, but it gave the other half a much more difficult set of questions. They had to think a lot, you know, put in more effort to answer the questions. So afterward, I didn't actually look at or grade anyone's work on the assignment, I just let everyone joined the group and watch the movie. And by the way, this movie that I had them watch, it was actually kind of boring, an old documentary. But I didn't say that and you know their reactions to the movie really demonstrated this idea we're talking about, because the students who had only answered easy questions for the assignment, well, they saw the movie for what it was, a boring old documentary, but the students who had to complete their difficult assignment in order to watch the movie, well, they tended to say they thought the movie was pretty good and interesting, which in light of this concept isn't really surprising, is it?

4. 词汇分析2

privilege /ˈprɪvəlɪdʒ/   *n*. 特权

psychological /ˌsaɪkəˈlɑːdʒɪkl/   *adj*. 心理的

a bunch of   一堆

put in more effort   付出更多的努力

tend to   有……的倾向

5. 范例答案

In the reading, effort justification means that if people work hard to attain or accomplish something, they tend to subconsciously justify or defend the effort they made, so that it seems worthwhile.

In the lecture, the professor gives an experiment he did to explain it. A few years ago, the professor set up a special discussion group about analyzing movies. He made it as a privilege to join the group and explained that interested students had to complete assignments first to show their ability of understanding psychological concepts.

Then the professor divided the students in two parts as easy or difficult assignments. The students in difficult part made more efforts to think. But he didn't look at the score, just let everyone in the group to watch the boring old documentary together.

And he found out that students' reaction really demonstrated the idea of effort justification. The students in easy part just thought it was boring, but the students with hard assignments thought it was a great and interesting movie.

十一、Call Matching

In certain animal species, the ability to identify fellow group members is important for survival. Resources held in common cannot be adequately shared and defended unless group members are able to interact and cooperate. However, certain animal species that live in large groups may not be able to visually recognize all other group members. Some of these species have developed a different method of identifying group members through call matching. Animals in such species learn to replicate and match the sound of their calls so that every member's call is identical. Even new animals that join the group learn to adjust their calls to be identifiable as a member and share in the group's resources.

1. 词汇分析 1

identify /aɪˈdentɪfaɪ/　*v*. 识别

adequately /ˈædɪkwətli/　*adv*. 适当地，充分地

visually /ˈvɪʒwəli/　*adv*. 看得见地

replicate /ˈreplɪkeɪt/　*v*. 重复，复制

identical /aɪˈdentɪkl/　*adj*. 完全相同的

2. 信息提取

Call matching refers to a method of identifying fellows for invisible species to learn to replicate and match the sound of their calls so that every member's call is identical.

3. 听力原文

So there is a particular type of bat in South America. That is a really good example. These bats live together in colonies and each colony may have hundreds of bats in it and there may be many different bat colonies living in a single cave and even more different bat colonies living nearby. Now the bats living in all these different colonies make these high-pitched noises or screeches when they fly around. But each colony has its own particular screeching noise. This is important when the bats are looking for fruit to eat because if one of the bats finds an area where lots of fruit is growing, it will let out a screech. And then other bats from its colony will fly toward the source of the sound and these other bats are making the same screech as the bat who discovered the fruit. It will know that it's okay to share the fruit with them.

But when bats from other different colonies hear all this screeching. Well, they won't do a thing because they know that the bats from the first colony are there and won't share the fruit with strangers. So even when female bats leave the colonies where they were born and eventually joined different colonies once they reach maturity. After a female bat joins a new colony, it may continue to make its old screeching noise from its old colony for a while, but eventually it changes and sounds like the other bats in the new colony, because otherwise it wouldn't be able to participate in activities like finding fruit, which is useful.

4. 词汇分析 2

high-pitched /ˌhaɪ ˈpɪtʃt/　*adj*. 声调高的

screech /skriːtʃ/　*v*. 尖叫

maturity /məˈtʃʊrəti/　*n*. 成熟

colony /ˈkɑːləni/　*n*. 群落

participate in　参与

5. 范例答案

Call matching refers to a method of identifying fellows for invisible species to learn to replicate and match the sound of their calls so that every member's call is identical.

In the lecture, the professor gives an example of bats to explain it. Hundreds of bats live together in the same colony, and there are more bats nearby. In the same colony, the bats would make high-pitched noises like screeching for their own participation.

Such behavior is important for finding fruits. When the first group of bats find fruits and make noises, the left ones in the same colony would recognize and fly to the source. They make same sound and it is ok to share. But the bats in different colony won't go without sharing.

Besides, when female bats leave the old group and join the new, they would remain their old sound matching. But eventually, they would change for better participation of fruits.

十二、Hurdle Help

When students are learning new skills or trying to complete new tasks, teachers generally encourage them to try to complete the tasks independently. However, a particular obstacle or portion of the task may be impossible for them to overcome without assistance, and thus students may become frustrated and stop trying. In such situations, teachers may use the technique of hurdle help, in which the teacher performs a particularly challenging part of a task for students, and then allows the students to complete the rest of the task independently. This ensures that students are able to complete the task and helps control students' classroom behavior.

1. 词汇分析1

hurdle /ˈhɜːrdl/ v. 跨栏；渡过难关

obstacle /ˈɑːbstəkl/ n. 障碍

portion /ˈpɔːrʃn/ n. 部分

assistance /əˈsɪstəns/ n. 帮助，援助

frustrate /ˈfrʌstreɪt/ v. 使懊恼，使沮丧

ensure /ɪnˈʃʊr/ v. 确保，保证

2. 信息提取

Hurdle help is a technique in which the teacher performs a particularly challenging part of a task for students, and then allows the students to complete the rest of the task independently.

3. 听力原文

So I've actually seen this while observing student-teachers, teachers in training, teaching a class. So this student-teacher was working with young children, five year old kids, and she was teaching them a lesson about animals that live in the forest and this part of the lesson, she wanted each student to cut out a picture of their favorite forest animal and pasted on a piece of paper. So while the class was working on this, the teacher was watching. And she noticed that a few students were having trouble cutting out the animals. They were not yet physically developed enough to use the scissors and cut around the shapes of the animals, so they kept making mistakes and accidentally cutting through the picture or cutting a shape that was too big, and so some of them just gave up on cutting out the animals and started talking to each other instead. This was distracting the rest of the class. Well, at this point, what the teacher did was to go around and cut out the shapes for the students having trouble cutting out the animals. Once she cut them, the students pasted them on paper, and that way the students stopped talking and disturbing the rest of the class, and the whole class was able to paste the pictures on paper.

4. 词汇分析 2

accidentally /ˌæksɪˈdɛntəli/　*adv*. 意外地,偶然地
physically-developed　身体发育

5. 范例答案

According to the passage, Hurdle help is a technique in which the teacher performs a particularly challenging part of a task for students, and then allows the students to complete the rest of the task independently.

The professor gives a story to explain the term. A student-teacher was working with some five-year-old kids, and she wanted each student to cut out a picture of their favorite forest animal and pasted on a piece of paper. She soon noticed that some students were not yet physically developed enough to use the scissors, so they kept making mistakes. They may accidentally cut through the picture or cutting a shape that was too big, so some of them just gave up. At this point, what the teacher did was to help cut out the shapes for those students. Once she cut them, the students pasted them on paper, and that way the students stopped disturbing the rest of the class.

十三、Freeloader Effect

Teamwork can be highly effective in both the workplace and the classroom. However, when team assignments are not carefully planned, some team members may become freeloaders, that is they may take advantage of the hard work of others and share in the team's success without contributing to it. This phenomenon is known as the freeloader effect. One way that managers and teachers can avoid the freeloader effect is by making each team member accountable for a particular part of the work that is being carried out by the team.

1. 词汇分析1

freeloader /ˈfriːloʊdər/   n. 在小组项目里不参与，坐等成绩的人

contribute /kənˈtrɪbjuːt/   v. 为……作出贡献

phenomenon /fəˈnaːmɪnən/   n. 现象

accountable /əˈkaʊntəbl/   adj. 有责任的

particular /pərˈtɪkjələr/   adj. 特定的

carry /ˈkæri/ v. 实行

2. 信息提取

Freeloader effect is a phenomenon which means that some students might take advantage of the hard work of others and then share in the team's success without contributing to it.

3. 听力原文

So I used to teach little kids in elementary school, and one of the things I had them do is read books and discuss them in groups. So they read the book on their own, but then I'd put four or five students together and have them work as a team to answer some questions I designed. I graded the assignment, and everyone in the team would get the same score. But over time, something I noticed was that in some of the groups there were two or three students who were talking about the book a lot and writing down the answers, but the others weren't participating at all. They just let the others do all the work, and this was unfair to the ones who did all the work, of course, and earned a good grade for the rest of the team members. I knew I had to do something to address this. So instead of just giving each group a list of questions to answer about the book, I started designing one question to each student in the group, so that student had to be the first one to respond to the question and tell the others what he or she thought about it. That way, each student had to be part of the discussion. And so they all started participating, even the students who hadn't been paying attention or talking about the questions before, and everyone learned something.

4. 词汇分析2

elementary /ˌelɪˈmentri/ adj. 简单的,基本的

address /əˈdres/　v. 解决

participate /pɑːrˈtɪsɪpeɪt/　v. 参加，参与

respond /rɪˈspɑːnd/　v. 回复

5. 范例答案

According to the passage, freeloader effect is a phenomenon which means that some students might take advantage of the hard work of others and then share in the team's success without contributing to it.

The professor gives his own class as an example and says that in the past, he used to assign book reading assignments to his students. After that students had to answer some questions as a team. However, he noticed that some students, like two or three of them, would talk a lot while the others were not pitching in and still get the same grade. He thought that it was not fair. So instead of the original plan, the professor assigned one question to each of the students who had to be the first to answer that question. In this way, each students had to be a part of the work. As a result, everyone started contributing and everyone learnt something.

十四、Population Bottlenecks

The overall health of a plant species is the strongest when the species has genetic variation—that is, when individual members of the population possess different inherited genetic traits and are not all the same. Genetic diversity increases the likelihood that at least some individual plants possess traits that help them resist disease. Sometimes, however, when an event known as a population bottleneck occurs, a previously large population is drastically reduced to a small number of individuals. The wide variety of genetic traits that the population previously had is narrowed to only the few characteristics present in the remaining plants. Therefore，subsequent generations of the species also lack genetic diversity and may be especially vulnerable to disease.

1. 词汇分析 1

genetic /dʒə'netɪk/　*adj*. 基因的，遗传学的；有共同起源的

variation /ˌveri'eɪʃn/　*n*. 变化，变动

possess /pə'zes/　*v*. 拥有，持有

inherited /ɪn'herɪtɪd/　*adj*.（疾病或特点）遗传的

trait /treɪt/　*n*. 特征，特点

drastically /'dræstɪkli/　*adv*. 极其，非常

2. 信息提取

Population bottleneck is an event in which a previously large population is drastically reduced to a small number of individuals. As a result，subsequent generations lack genetic diversity and may be especially vulnerable to disease.

3. 听力原文

So let me give you a historical example of this involving the potato.

Now potatoes were originally cultivated by farmers in South America，and farmers there grew many different shapes, colors and sizes of potatoes. Well，when Europeans colonized South America hundreds of years ago，they tried potatoes and like them，and they decided to bring back some potatoes to Europe and start growing them there. But... um... and this is important，they didn't bring back very many of the potatoes，just a small number of plants of the specific size and color they like the most. And so almost all European potatoes that were grown after that were descendants of those few initial plants that the Europeans brought back on their ships from South America. And this had an important effect because... well, in the 1800s a fungus called the potato blight started to attack potatoes and spread around the world. European potatoes have been growing well and became an important crop there, but when the potato blight reached Europe and this fungus began attacking European potatoes, well, because of what we've been talking about, none of the European potato plants were able to fight off the blight, and so a lot of potato crops throughout Europe were completely destroyed, which caused widespread food shortages.

Now the blight also affected potato crops in South America, and some plants there were killed by the blight, but others were able to fight it off and didn't die. And so overall South American potatoes recovered quite well from the blight, unlike potatoes in Europe.

4. 词汇分析2

distracting /dɪˈstræktɪŋ/ *adj*. 分心的；分散注意力的
disturb /dɪˈstɜːrb/ *v*. 打扰，妨碍

5. 范例答案

According to the passage, population bottleneck is an event in which a previously large population is drastically reduced to a small number of individuals. As a result, subsequent generations lack genetic diversity and may be especially vulnerable to disease.

The professor gives potato as an example to explain the term. Potatoes were originally cultivated by farmers in South America and later brought to Europe. They didn't bring back very many of the potatoes, just a small number of plants of the specific size and color they like the most. What happened was, in the 1800s a fungus called the potato blight started to attack potatoes and spread around the world. So when the potato blight reached Europe, a lot of potato crops throughout Europe were completely destroyed, which caused widespread food shortages. As we can see, the blight also affected potato crops in South America, but some potatoes survived because of the genetic variation.

十五、Social Referencing

A young baby is continually exposed to new situations but only later develops the ability to understand new situations and learn how to respond. Psychologists refer to this ability as social referencing. It does not develop until around the age of one. A child capable of social referencing looks at other people, like parents, for emotional signals that indicate what a new situation means and how the child should respond to it. Typically, the signals are facial expressions that express attitudes about the situation. While very young babies do not react to such signals, one-year-old children do seem to understand them and subsequently behave in ways that reflect the parent's attitude.

1. 词汇分析 1

referencing /ˈrefrənsɪŋ/　*n*. 参考,引用

capable /ˈkeɪpəbl/　*adj*. 有能力的

indicate /ˈɪndɪkeɪt/　*v*. 表示

emotional /ɪˈmoʊʃənl/　*adj*. 情绪的

react /riˈækt/　*v*. 反应

signal /ˈsɪgnəl/　*v*. 标志,预示

subsequently /ˈsʌbsɪkwəntli/　*adv*. 随后,后来

facial expression　面部表情

2. 信息提取

Social referencing is an ability for kids to understand new situations and learn to respond to them. So usually, this ability doesn't develop until the age of one.

3. 听力原文

So in a recent experiment researchers asked mothers to offer their six-month-old babies new toy dolls to play with, some of the mothers were told to smile at the dolls while other mothers were told to frown at the dolls. What happened?

Well, all the six-month-old babies immediately started playing with the dolls, regardless of whether their mothers were smiling or frowning. Then the researchers did the same experiment with a group of older children who were one year old.

Again, each of the mother's held a new doll, some smiling at their dolls and others frowning at them. But this time, with the older children, the response was quite different, when the smiling mothers offer the dolls to their children, the children readily took the dolls and started playing with them right away. But when the frowning mothers offered the dolls to their children, the children avoided the dolls and would not play with them at all. So, unlike the six-month-old babies, the older children first stopped to notice how their mothers reacted to the dolls, and then the children reacted exactly the same way.

4. 词汇分析2

immediately /ɪˈmiːdiətli/   *adv*. 立即,马上

regardless /rɪˈgɑːrdləs/   *adv*. 不顾,不加理会

frown /fraʊn/   *v*. 皱眉

readily /ˈredɪli/   *adv*. 轻而易举地,迅速地

5. 范例答案

According to the passage，social referencing is an ability for kids to understand new situations and learn to respond to them. So usually，this ability doesn't develop until the age of one.

In the lecture the professor gives an example to explain this term. In the example，the mothers offered toy dolls for their kids to play. And for the first set of experiment，there are six-month-old kids，some moms would smile at the dolls，while some were frowning. What happened was，no matter which face the mom made，the kids would always start playing immediately regardless of the facial expression. And then in the second set of experiments，they were doing it with one-year-old kids. Again，some moms were smiling and the others were frowning. This time the responses were very different for the frowning mothers. Their kids avoided playing the dolls at all. Unlike the six-month-old kids，the older children first noticed the situation and then reacted to it.

第十五章 Task 4

一、题目 1

1. 题目要求

Using examples from the lecture，explain two characteristics of effective teachers.

2. 听力原文

So we've been talking about how good teaching helps students learn. But what are some of the characteristics of an effective teacher?

Well，according to research，one important characteristic is that teachers maintain a supportive attitude towards their students. Now，what does it mean to have a supportive attitude?

Well，it means encouraging students，rather than penalizing them. Good teachers build confidence in their students by showing that they themselves have confidence in student performance. And they praise students for what they do rather than stressing what students do wrong. For example，I had a geometry teacher in high school and his name was Mr. Randall. And even when I told him what a terrible math student I was on the first day of class, he kept right on encouraging me: keep working hard, you're going to do a lot better than you think. He told me and that really helped improve my own attitude and gave me confidence that maybe I could solve difficult math problems after all.

But maintaining a supportive attitude isn't the only important trait, researchers say that the most effective teachers also provide regular almost immediate feedback to their students. That kind of prompt response to student helps to clear up any misunderstanding students may have right away. So that mistakes won't be repeated. Mr. Randall, the geometry teacher, he graded and returned all our homework assignments immediately. So that we always had them back by the end of each day that helped to reinforce each new lesson taught in class, so we would understand and remember the correct way to do geometry problems. And by the time the course was over, I ended up with a much better geometer grade than I'd expected.

3. 范例答案

In the lecture, the professor mainly talks about characteristics of effective teachers.

The first characteristic is that good teachers maintain a supportive attitude towards their students.

The example is a geometry teacher the professor had in high school. The professor was a terrible math student at that time. The teacher kept on encouraging him like: keep working hard, you're going to do a lot better than you think. He told the professor and really helped improve his own attitude and gave him confidence.

The second characteristic is that effective teachers also provide immediate feedback to their students.

And the example is still the geometry teacher, he graded and returned all homework assignments immediately. So that students always had them back by the end of each day that helped to reinforce each new lesson taught in class. Students would understand and remember the correct way to do geometry problems. And by the time the course was over, the professor ended up with a much better geometer grade than he'd expected.

二、题目 2

1. 题目要求

Using points and examples from the lecture, explain two situations where teamwork can be ineffective.

2. 听力原文

Listen to part of a lecture from a business class.

So we've been talking about ways that businesses can organize workers, to make the business more successful. And we start discussing teamwork, when employees work together on assignments instead of alone.

Now, having several people work as a group or team can often contribute to the success of a business, and is usually seen as a good business practice. In certain situations, however, teamwork can be ineffective. Let's consider two of these situations.

First of all, when a team begins work on a project, compromise is a must. A group of people coming together, each individual can't get his or her own way, right? You have to share your opinion and maybe adjust it, decide with others how a project is to be done for the good of the project. So if someone won't accept other people's views and opinions on a matter, and he's unwilling to compromise, this may prevent the team from being productive and accomplishing the goal of the project. Consider a team of architects, working on the design of a new building. If one architect wants the building to look more modern, and refuses to compromise with other architects on the team who want the building to look more traditional, it may prevent the project from moving forward.

Teamwork can also be ineffective when there's a task that needs to be completed quickly, by a specific date or deadline. Teamwork can make some assignments take longer because well teamwork takes time. It takes time for multiple people to meet, communicate, and come to a decision. For example, if it's a team of editors on a newspaper who have to decide which articles to publish, the newspaper might not be ready by the deadline, because of the time it takes for all the editors to get together and decide on which articles to include.

3. 范例答案

In the lecture, the professor uses two examples to explain two situations where teamwork can be ineffective.

First of all, in a team project, compromise is a must. In the group, each individual has to share opinion and adjust it. So if someone won't accept other people's views and opinions, and unwilling to compromise, this may prevent the team from being productive and accomplishing the goal of the project. For example, a team of architects are designing a new building. If one architect wants the building more modern, and refuses to compromise with other architects who want the building more traditional, it may prevent the project from moving forward.

Second, teamwork can also be ineffective when the task needs to be completed quickly, by a specific date or deadline. Teamwork can make the assignments longer because it takes time for people to meet, communicate, and come to a decision. For example, if a team of editors need to decide which articles to publish, the newspaper might not be ready by the deadline, because the time for all the editors to get together and decide is long.

三、题目 3

1. 题目要求

Using points and examples from the lecture，explain two ways that music changed after the invention of recording technology.

2. 听力原文

Listen to part of a lecture from a music history class.

Okay，so today we are talking about how music was influenced by the invention of recording technology.

For most of human history，of course，there was no way to record music and listen to it again later. All music was performed in front of a live audience. When recording technology appeared，musicians were eager to preserve their music and to get it to a wider audience. And actually，the use of recording technology led to some changes in the way that musicians made their music.

First of all，musicians had to change their music to keep it within the limits of what the new recording technology could do. I am sure it's hard to imagine now，but early records could only hold about three minutes of music. So before recording technology was invented，musicians could write really long songs if they wanted to. They didn't have to worry about whether their songs might be too long to be recorded. Live audiences don't have a time limit. So for example，musicians will often use repetition in music，though repeat the same sequence of notes several times within a song with some small variation, but when the record came along, musicians started writing music with fewer repetitions, so that an entire song could fit on the recording.

Now, it wasn't all limitations, recording technology also allowed musicians to experiment with new styles of sound in their music. Before recording technology, musicians played in big rooms and they had to sing loudly so that everyone could hear them. The invention of the microphone made it possible to record very quiet music for people to listen to in their homes. That gave musicians new ideas. For example, some singers in the United States began to sing in a style called crooning, where they sang directly into microphones in soft, quiet tones. Their recordings had a brand-new sound, a soft, intimate sound, like the listener was standing right next to the singer.

3. 范例答案

In the lecture, the professor uses two examples to explain two ways that music changed after the invention of recording technology.

First of all, musicians had to keep their music within the limits of the new recording technology could do. Early records could only hold about three minutes. So before recording technology was invented, musicians could write long songs because live audiences don't have a time limit. For example, musicians will often repeat the same sequence of notes several times with some small variation, but when they needed to record, they wrote music with fewer repetitions, so that an entire song could fit on the recording.

Second, recording technology also allowed musicians to experiment with new styles of sound. Before recording technology, musicians played in big rooms, so they had to sing loudly to make everyone hear them. The invention of the microphone let them record quiet music for people to listen to in their homes. For example, some singers in the United States began to sing crooning. They sang directly into microphones in quiet tones and had a soft, intimate sound, like the listener was standing next to the singer.

四、题目 4

1. 题目要求

Using points and examples from the lecture, explain two ways prairie dogs benefit their ecosystem.

2. 听力原文

Listen to part of a lecture in an environmental science class.

So, we started talking about the prairies or grasslands in North America. These open areas are home to many species of animals, and certain species like the prairie dog play a very important role in the grassland ecosystem. You see, prairie dogs dig burrows. They dig holes in the soil, tunnels where they live and hide from predators. And while these burrows are, of course, necessary for the prairie dogs to live in, they're actually also really important for this surrounding environment, the grasslands. So, um... prairie dogs and their burrows benefit the grassland ecosystem.

One benefit is that the prairie dogs' burrows provide a habitat for other animals, a kind of shelter they can use. Prairie dogs dig their burrows for protection from predators. And when a prairie dog is no longer using a burrow, well, it can provide those same benefits for other animals that don't dig their own burrows but may take over an abandoned prairie dog's burrow. For example, there is a type of owl. These birds build nests inside empty burrows that the prairie dogs are not using anymore, and it helps keep the young owls safe since their hidden underground rather than being exposed on the open prairie.

Also, the actual act of constructing a burrow, you know, when they're digging a burrow, it helps keep the soil suitable for plant growth. When prairie dogs dig tunnels, it improves the condition of the soil, because it moves the soil around a lot and loosens it up. And loosening up the soil allows it to soak up a good amount of water when it rains, which is good for plants. So to give you an idea of this, researchers have noticed that there are thicker tufts of grass growing from the soil above prairie dogs' burrows. The grasses grow much better in the soil near the burrows.

3. 范例答案

In the lecture, the professor uses two examples to explain two ways prairie dogs benefit their ecosystem.

First benefit is the burrows provide a habitat for other animals as a shelter. Prairie dogs dig their burrows for protection from predators. But when a prairie dog is no longer using a burrow, it can provide benefits for other animals. They don't dig their own burrows but may take over an abandoned prairie dog's burrow. For example, owl will build nests inside the empty burrows and it helps keep the young owls safe since their hidden underground rather than being exposed on the open prairie.

Secondly, constructing a burrow can help keep the soil suitable for plant growth. When prairie dogs dig tunnels, it moves the soil around a lot and loosens it up, and soil can soak up a lot of water when it rains, which is good for plants. Researchers have noticed there are thicker tufts of grass growing above the burrows. The grasses grow much better in the soil near the burrows.

五、题目5

1. 题目要求

Using points and examples of the maple tree and the avocado tree, describe two ways in which shedding benefits plants.

2. 听力原文

Listen to part of a lecture in a biology class.

All right, so let's look at another form of plant behavior—shedding. Some plants shed... um, drop some of their parts. The parts that plants commonly drop are leaves, flowers, seeds and fruits. And for many plants species, this behavior, shedding, benefits them in several ways. Let's look at some good effects that shedding has for plants.

First, shedding can prevent damage to plants. Take the maple tree for example. It grows in climates where it's cold and snow falls during part of the year. At the approach of the cold season, the maple tree begins to shed its leaves. Its leaves begin to fall to the ground. So how does this prevent damage to the maple tree? Well, if the leaves remained on the tree, snow would fall on them and turn into ice, and the snow and ice would continue to build up throughout the season. Under the weight of all the snow and ice, the branches would begin to break and cause damage to the tree. So by shedding its leaves, the tree avoids this kind of damage.

Now，um … Other plants benefit in a different way from shedding their parts. They're able to conserve nutrients. The avocado tree is a good example of a plant that benefits in this way from shedding. The avocado tree usually produces large numbers of young fruit，and the young fruit needs lots of nutrients to grow and develop into mature fruit. But since the avocado tree produces much more fruit than it can nourish to maturity，what it does is to shed some of its fruit，allowing some of it to fall to the ground. So the tree no longer has to nourish the fallen fruit and it can save enough nutrients to let the remaining fruit develop into maturity.

3. 范例答案

In the lecture，the professor uses two examples to explain two ways that shedding can benefit plants.

First，shedding can prevent damage. For example，maple tree grows in cold and snow climate. In cold season，maple tree would shed its leaves and let the leaves fall to the ground. Because if leaves remained on the tree，snow would fall on them and turn into ice，and they would continue to build up through the season. Under the weight of snow and ice，branches would break and cause damage to the tree. So by shedding leaves，the tree avoids this damage.

Second，shedding can conserve nutrients for the tree. For example，avocado tree usually produces large number of young fruits and they need lots of nutrients to grow and mature. But the tree produces so many fruits that they cannot nourish to maturity. So it would shed some of the fruits and allow them to fall to the ground and it can save enough nutrients to let the remaining fruit develop into maturity.

六、题目 6

1. 题目要求

Using points and examples from the lecture, explain two ways oxygen is replenished in water.

2. 听力原文

Listen to part of a lecture in a biology class.

So we've been talking about lakes and rivers and animals that live in these freshwater environments. Now, an important requirement for these animals is oxygen. They need oxygen to breathe, just like we do. And at any given time, there's oxygen present in the water which the animals breathe, but the animals use up oxygen as they breathe, so it has to be continually replenished or replaced. So where does the new oxygen come from? Well, the oxygen in water is replenished in a couple of different ways.

First, some of the oxygen in lakes and rivers is produced by internal sources within the body of water itself. Certain organisms in the water create oxygen as a byproduct or secondary effect of their normal activities, and the oxygen they create gets released into the water. For example, plants in a lake use sunlight to produce energy, and this process creates oxygen that is then released into the water, and the animals in the lake use that oxygen to breathe.

Now, oxygen also enters the water from external sources. The surrounding air contains oxygen and it can enter through the surface of the water, where the water is in contact with the air. This provides some oxygen, but it can be replenished even faster under certain conditions. When more water is in contact with the air, more oxygen can pass through these surfaces and dissolve into the water. For example, when the wind blows over a lake, the water rises up into waves, and these waves provide more surfaces for the water to be in contact with the air, which in turn, provides more oxygen for the animals in the lake.

3. 范例答案

In the lecture, the professor uses two examples to explain two ways oxygen is replenished in water.

First, oxygen is produced by internal sources within the body of water itself. Certain organisms can create oxygen as a byproduct or secondary effect of their activities, and they release the oxygen into the water. For example, plants in a lake use sunlight to produce energy, and creates oxygen that is released into the water, for animals to breathe.

Second, oxygen also enters the water from external sources. The surrounding air contains oxygen and it can enter through the surface of the water. When water is in contact with the air, it provides some oxygen, and it can be replenished faster under certain conditions. When more water is in contact, more oxygen can pass through the surfaces and dissolve into water. For example, when the wind blows over a lake, the waves can provide more surfaces for the water to be in contact with the air, which in turn, provides more oxygen for the lake animals.

七、题目 7

1. 题目要求

Summarize the professor's lecture about how spiders use mimicry. Be sure to include both the example of the moths and the example of the jumping spiders.

2. 听力原文

Some animals have the ability to mimic or copy other animals. And sometimes predators use this ability to lure in and catch their prey. Prey animals normally don't want to get anywhere near one of their predators, for obvious reasons. But if the predators are mimicking another type of animal, their prey might be deceived, tricked into getting close enough to the predator to be caught, spiders, for instance. Spiders use a couple different kinds of mimicry to help them catch their prey. So, first of all, many animals emit chemicals that have a particular smell. And the animals use these odors to recognize other animals. Now certain spiders have evolved the ability to mimic these smells or the odors of other animals by emitting chemicals that smell similar to the chemicals emitted by their prey, which has the effect of attracting their prey. So the prey will be drawn toward the odor, and then the spider can catch them. For example, a spider that cats moths can emit an odor that smells just like a female moth. So male moths thinking they found a female moth, fly straight to the spider. OK, now some spiders hunt and prey on other spiders, and they are effective at this by mimicking the prey of the spiders they're hunting. Acting like they are the prey by mimicking their physical actions in order to lure the spider they are hunting in order to eat them. For example, jumping spiders hunt web building spiders by pretending to be caught in the web building spiders' web, moving around like it's struggling in the web in order to grab the attention of the web building spider. So the web building spider goes over to investigate, thinking is called a meal, and I bet you can guess what happens next.

3. 范例答案

In the lecture, the professor introduces two kinds of mimicry that spiders use to catch prey.

The first kind is to mimic the smell of prey by releasing similar chemicals. In the professor's example of the spider, its prey is the moth. So the spider would emit the same odor just like a female prey. So the male prey would think it is a mate and fly straight to the spider.

The second kind is to mimic the behavior that prey is hunting for. And the professor gives an example of jumping spider. It hunts the web building spider, and it would mimic like it is struggling in the web like the prey of web building spider. So the web building spider would investigate and think it is a meal to approach.

八、题目 8

1. 题目要求

Using the examples of the skunk cabbage and the lotus flower, explain two benefits of thermoregulation in plants.

2. 听力原文

In a biology class. As you probably already know, many animals can regulate their body temperature. Even if it's very cold outside, they use what's called thermoregulation to keep their internal body temperature within a comfortable range. But did you know that certain plants use thermoregulation too? In plants, this ability is beneficial for a couple of reasons. If the weather gets very cold, many plants start to freeze which damages the structure of their cells, eventually the entire plant might die. But some plants can control their temperature using thermoregulation so they can prevent this damage. For example, a plant called the skunk cabbage sprouts early in the spring, when it's still cold and snowy. While other plants leaves might freeze and their flowers might fall off, the skunk cabbage stays alive in the cold by keeping its leaves and flowers warm. It can even melt nearby snow because of the heat it generates. Thermoregulation also helps plants to reproduce. Many plants need to attract insects to do this. Insects land on the plant and get covered in pollen, and carry the pollen to another plant allowing that plant to be fertilized. Plant thermoregulation helps plants attract insects that will pollinate them because insects are attracted to warmth. For example, the lotus flower attracts insects by keeping itself warm. The insects actually need warmth to fly. So when it's cold they seek out the warm lotus plants and land on them. This is good for the lotus flower, because the visiting insects warm up, get covered in pollen and then fly off to other lotus plants.

3. 范例答案

In the lecture, the professor introduces two benefits of plants' thermoregulation.

The first point is to prevent damage of freezing inner cells when it is cold. And the professor takes skunk cabbage as an example. It sprouts in earlier spring that is also very cold. When the flowers of other plants fall off, the skunk cabbage could still keep alive by keeping its flowers and leaves warm. Its heat can still melt the snow.

The second point is to help plants reproduce by attracting pollinating insects. The professor gives an example of lotus flower. It can keep the warmth that is also needed by insects to fly. When it is cold the insects seek warmth and land on the lotus. It is beneficial since the visiting insects get covered and fly off to other plants.

九、题目 9

1. 题目要求

Using points and examples from the lecture, explain two reasons why a group of people might not adopt a cultural novelty.

2. 听力原文

So throughout history, ideas have spread from one culture to another. When different groups of people came into contact, they'd introduce new ideas to each other, ideas for new foods, new inventions, new ways of doing things. Researchers call these new ideas cultural novelties. When groups of people were exposed to cultural novelties, they sometimes adopt them, make them part of their own culture, but other times for various reasons, they wouldn't adopt them, why not?

Well, one reason is that groups would sometimes not adopt a cultural novelty had to do with the availability of materials. If it would be difficult for the group to obtain materials associated with the novelty，the group would be much less likely to adopt the novelty，even if they loved it，they would not be likely to incorporate it into their culture if it required materials that were not readily available to them. Like，one day a traveler comes to your country，just as a hypothetical example，and introduces a tasty soup recipe，and he makes the soup using spices he brought with him if those spices are not readily available in your country，that soup probably won't become part of your regular diet.

Another reason groups with sometimes not adopt a cultural novelty was they already had something similar in their own culture，something that could serve pretty much the same function as the cultural novelty. So in a sense，the novelty had to compete with something that was already well established，and in many cases，rather than adopt the novelty，the group would choose to stay with what they already had. Like，again，if travelers come along from another land and introduces stringed musical instrument to your culture，but you already have your own stringed instrument that everyone likes，that makes a similar sound，well，you would not start using that new instrument.

3. 范例答案

In the lecture，the professor introduces two reasons that people would not adopt cultural novelties.

The first reason is that the materials are not available in the own country. And the professor gives an example of soup recipe. Assume a traveler comes to a new area and introduces a new and tasty soup recipe. But the spices he brings are not available in the new area，so people would not use it in their regular diet.

The second reason is that there are similar things functioned the same in the country. Then the professor gives an example of stringed musical instrument. If a traveler comes to a new area and brings the stringed musical instrument，but it already exists in the culture and everybody likes the sound it makes. So due to the similar sound，people would not use the new one.

十、题目 10

1. 题目要求

Using points and examples from the lecture, explain two reasons why animals behave differently in captivity than in the wild.

2. 听力原文

So we've been talking about how researchers study animal behavior. And as you know, researchers observe animals both in the wild and in captivity, in places like zoos. Now it's important to be aware that when researchers observed the behaviors of a species of animal in captivity, they tend to see differences in behavior from what the animals do in the wild. And there are a couple of different reasons why animals behave differently in captivity than in the wild.

So one reason why researchers think animals' behavior is different in captivity is that they don't have the same survival needs. You know, they don't need to search for food, and they don't really have to worry about predators so they can spend less time on those things and more time doing other things, so the frequency of certain behaviors changes. For example, researchers have found that chimpanzees in captivity spend less time looking for food, and more time resting and playing.

Researchers think animals' behavior in captivity may also be the result of differences between their natural habitats and the captive environment, even though captive environments try to recreate animals' wild habitats, they're not exactly the

same. Conditions are slightly different, and so animals may respond to these differences in their environment by changing their behaviors and exhibiting in new behaviors in captivity, and these behaviors they don't normally show in the wild. For example, back to chimpanzees. In the wild, female chimpanzees are not particularly social, they keep to themselves, which may be because they have plenty of space to spread out. But in captivity, when chimpanzees live closer together and live in smaller spaces, the females become kind of social, they start engaging in behaviors like grooming or cleaning each other's fur.

3. 范例答案

In the lecture, the professor explains two reasons why animals behave differently in captivity than in the wild.

The first reason is that there is no survival needs for food or predators, animals would do other things. And the professor gives an example of chimpanzees. In captivity, chimpanzees spend less time on finding food, but they spend more time on resting or playing.

And the second reason is the difference between natural habitat and captivity environment. In the same example, in the wild, the female chimpanzees tend to less socialize with each other since they have plenty of spaces. But in captivity, with closer distance, they are more likely to socialize like grooming and cleaning the fur.

十一、题目 11

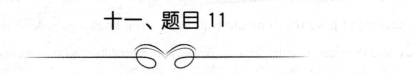

1. 题目要求

Using points and examples from the lecture describe the problem of rainwater runoff and explain two solutions to it.

2. 听力原文

So cities tend to have some problems with pollution. Of course, because of industry, manufacturing and a lot of people living close together. One issue for cities that are located near rivers is rainwater runoff. So when there is a storm, a sudden down pour of rain, that water accumulate on the city street and mix it with toxic substances there, like trash, oil or chemicals. The water picks up and carries these toxic substances into city drains, which empty into the river and the toxic substances will end up in the river. It's bad for the environment, so recently cities have been finding ways to address this problem of rainwater runoff. One solution is to find a way to prevent rainwater from collecting on the surface of the city streets. How do you do that? Well, the material the streets are made of is traditionally hard pavement, right? which doesn't exactly allow the rainwater to soak into the ground. So one solution involves changing the material that streets are made of.

For example, some cities are using a type of material that's full of very tiny holes that allow water to pass through the street to the ground. The material is still hard enough to support the weight of traffic but also porous enough that water can pass through.

Another solution involves reducing the amount of rainwater that actually makes it to the city street in the first place by capturing some of it before it hits the ground. Reducing the amount of water that reaches the street means that less water ends up running into city drains and going into the river and people can reuse the captured water for other purposes.

For example, officials in one city give each household a big rain barrel, a big container to put outside their house. So when it rains, water runs off the roof of the house and is directed into this barrel, instead of collecting on the ground. And that water can be reused for gardening or watering lawns.

3. 范例答案

In the lecture, the professor explains two ways of solving rainwater runoff in the city.

The first way is to prevent rainwater from collecting on the surface of city streets, to change the pavement materials. And the professor gives an example, some cities use the materials that full of tiny holes. So the water could pass through to the ground. This material is not only hard enough for supporting traffic, but porous to let water pass.

The second way is reducing the amount of water at first, to capture it and reuse it.

And the professor gives an example, the officials in the city would give each household a rain barrel to put outside the house. So the water from roof could be directed to barrel and reused for gardening or watering.

十二、题目 12

1. 题目要求

Using the examples of the two ectotherms, the tortoise and the frog. Explain how each can survive in extreme environments.

2. 听力原文

So we've been talking about how animals control their body temperature, but there is a group of animals called ectotherms that have no internal way of physiologically controlling their temperature. The outside temperature completely determines how warm or cold their bodies are. Some ectotherms live in extremely hot or cold environments, so they have unique adaptations to help them survive.

Ectotherms that live in very hot environments need ways to stay cool, so many of them create burrows, holes or tunnels underneath the ground that they can live in. They have legs adapted to digging into the soil, and the temperature is cooler underground than on the surface which is exposed to the hot sun. So, for example, this turtle or tortoise, the desert tortoise, lives in hot deserts. It has strong front legs with large, sharp claws that make it easy to dig an underground burrow that it can keep cooling.

Ectotherms that live in extremely cold places have developed ways to survive. Some of them can actually become completely frozen in cold temperatures. They can remain frozen for months at a time but still stay alive. Their body fluids freeze, and most of their internal organs stopped performing their usual function. But then when the temperature rises, they warm up and their organs start functioning again, and the ectotherms resume its normal activities. For example, a type of frog that is found in areas with very cold winters. When it gets very cold, the drop in temperature triggers the production of a special substance inside the frog that protects the frog's cells from damage while its frozen, until spring, when the frog warms up and starts hopping around again.

3. 范例答案

In the lecture, the professor talks about how ectotherms can survive in extreme environments.

The first way is to create burrows, holes or tunnels underneath the ground that they can live in. The example is the desert tortoise. It lives in hot deserts. It has strong front legs with large, sharp claws that make it easy to dig an underground burrow. The temperature is cooler underground than on the surface which is exposed to the hot sun.

The second way is to become completely frozen in cold temperatures. The example is a type of frog. When it gets very cold, the drop in temperature triggers the production of a special substance inside the frog that protects the frog's cells from damage while its frozen, until spring, when the frog warms up and starts hopping around again.

十三、题目 13

1. 题目要求

Using the professor's points and examples, summarize the lecture about caterpillars.

2. 听力原文

We've been talking about insects and how they defend themselves from predators, and a particularly interesting case is that of butterflies. Well, especially caterpillars, the larvae of butterflies. They're not butterflies yet, they're still in the larval stage, which means they're not yet fully mature or grown. Now, if you've seen a caterpillar, you know that it doesn't move quickly, it hasn't developed wings yet, so it can't fly. It just crawls around slowly on plants, eating leaves. If a predator attacks a caterpillar, the caterpillars are vulnerable, because it can't get away from the predator quickly. So caterpillars have developed different ways of defending themselves against predators in order to survive their early larval stage. So these slow moving caterpillars may have special defensive features on their bodies, physical features that make it difficult or impossible for predators to attack and eat them. And if predators have to make too much effort trying to eat their prey, they will avoid that type of prey in the future.

For example, there is a species of caterpillar with thousands of tiny rough hairs on his body. Most birds that try to eat this hairy caterpillar have a hard time swallowing it because of all the hair. So these birds will probably leave the caterpillar alone and not try to eat it in the future.

How else do caterpillars defend themselves?

Well, this may sound strange, but another thing they do is they get other animals to protect them. The caterpillar attracts other insects to it, and these other insects protect the caterpillar from predators, but the other insects get something in return. For example, some caterpillars produce a sweet liquid that attracts ants, the ants drink this liquid off the caterpillar's bodies. And since the ants want to protect their food source, if predators come near, the ants bite them and chase them away before they can harm the caterpillars.

3. 范例答案

In the lecture, the professor explains two ways caterpillars defend themselves from predators. So caterpillars are slow-moving insects, they can't fly, and they are always crawling slowly on leaf. So they're vulnerable.

The first way they defend themselves is to develop some physical features. The caterpillars have thousands of tiny rough hairs, so when the bird tried to eat them, they will be having a hard time swallowing the caterpillars because all those little hairs. The next time they see a caterpillar, they will leave it alone and not try to eat them again.

The second way birds defend themselves is to get other insects to help them. Caterpillars produce a kind of sweet liquid that ants like to drink. Ants love this kind of liquid. So in order to protect their food source, the ants would chase away whatever predator that might try to eat them.

十四、题目 14

1. 题目要求

Using points and examples from the lecture, explain two reasons why a company might change a product's packaging.

2. 听力原文

A product packaging, the container it's stored and sold in, is actually a very important part of the product and its marketing, so companies spend a lot of time deciding what kind of packaging to use. Sometimes after a company has been selling a product for a while, it may decide to change the product's packaging, offer the same product in a new redesigned container.

Why would a company do this? Well, let's talk about two reasons.

One reason a company might change their product's packaging is in response to new technology, like the invention of better material. As technology improves, new materials are invented, and better ways of packaging products may emerge. For instance, when milk was first being marketed in the United States, it was mostly sold in glass bottles, but this was expensive since glass costs a lot and is fragile. If you accidentally drop the glass bottle it would break and make a mass. With the invention of plastic, however, a new material became available that was cheaper and more durable because plastic did not break as easily as glass. So to take advantage of this new technology, some companies started selling milk and plastic containers.

Another reason a company might change a product's packaging is to better compete with other companies to make the packaging more competitive with the packaging of other products. Sometimes this is done by changing the size of the package. So back to our milk example, the bottles that milk were originally sold in were large. They were large containers, but now you also see milk being sold in small portable containers. Why this change to a smaller container? Well, because other competing companies producing beverages like juices, teas or soft drinks were selling them in smaller, more portable containers that people could take to work with them or drink in the car. So to compete, milk companies also started selling milk in smaller portable containers.

3. 范例答案

In the lecture, the professor talks about two reasons why a company might change a product's packaging.

The first reason is to response to new technology, like the invention of better material. In the example, professor says that when milk was first being marketed in the United States, it was mostly sold in glass bottles, but this was expensive since glass costs a lot and is fragile. With the invention of plastic, people can see that it was cheaper and more durable. So to take advantage of this new technology, some companies started selling milk and plastic containers.

The second reason is to better compete with other companies to make the packaging more competitive with the packaging of other products. Back to the milk example, the milk bottles were originally large. However, because other competing companies producing beverages like juices, teas or soft drinks were selling them in smaller, more portable containers, milk companies also started selling milk in smaller portable containers, just to be competitive.

十五、题目 15

1. 题目要求

Using the examples of the musk ox and the arctic tern, explain two ways animals cooperate to protect themselves.

2. 听力原文

Animals have different behaviors to defend themselves.

Defensive behaviors exhibited by individual animals, it's also exhibited by groups of animals. So animals cooperate, they work in groups in order to protect themselves or their young from potential predators. Together they are able to accomplish more than a single animal could achieve alone. Now, one way animals cooperate for the protection of the group is by encircling their young. They form a protective circle around their young, when they are threatened by a predator.

Musk ox are great example of this, when they're threatened by a predator such as a wolf, the adults in the herd will cooperate by gathering in a circle, all adults facing outward, with their young calves in the middle. If the wolf approaches the group, what will happen is, an adult ox or two will charge from the circle running at the wolf in an attempt to drive it off. The vacant spot left by those who went forward would be filled by the other oxen, closing the circle behind them. They tighten the circle, and thus the defensive ring stays secure and keeps the young protected. A single musk ox, of course, could not do any of this alone.

Now, a second way animals, particularly birds, cooperate to protect themselves is called mobbing. For example, there's a type of bird called arctic tern, these birds now live in large colonies, and they are very aggressive, very protective of their territory. Then terns spot a predator, such as a fox, intruding on their territory. They will attack the fox crying loudly and diving continually at the invaders' head, this behavior, this mobbing by the whole group of terns, usually results in the fox leaving the area. By mobbing, arctic terns can drive off of much larger predators than a single bird could by itself.

3. 范例答案

In the lecture, the professor talks about two ways animal cooperate to protect themselves.

The first way is by encircling the young. The professor gives musk ox as an example and says that when a wolf is trying to attack their young, the adults gather to form a circle around those kids. And then if the wolf doesn't leave, one or two adults would charge at the wolf and try to drive the wolf off. The vacant spot left by those who went forward would be filled, so the young were protected in this way.

The second way animals cooperate to protect themselves is by mobbing. This usually happens to birds, the professor gives arctic terns as an example and says that they live in large colonies and they are very protective when they spot a fox, they would attack the fox and diving continually at the fox's head and they would drive it off.